The Working Guide to
to
Traditional
Small-Boat Sails

The Working Guide to Traditional Small-Boat Sails

A How-To Handbook
for Builders and Owners

DAVID L. NICHOLS

BREAKAWAY BOOKS
HALCOTTSVILLE, NEW YORK
2006

The Working Guide to Traditional Small-Boat Sails:
A How-To Handbook for Owners and Builders

Copyright 2006 by David L. Nichols

ISBN-10: 1-891369-67-9
ISBN-13: 978-1-891369-67-4
Library of Congress Control Number: 2006926642

Published by Breakaway Books
P.O. Box 24
Halcottsville, NY 12438
www.breakawaybooks.com

SECOND PRINTING: JANUARY 2009

ACKNOWLEDGMENTS

To my wife, Candy; to my family and my friends: Without your steadfast support, sound editorial advice, and thoughtful connections, this book would not exist. Thank you, from the bottom of my heart, thank you.

CONTENTS

This book is dedicated to the fond memory of
Edward Everett Hale IV,
friend and mentor,
who introduced me to traditional sails
and showed me their value.

1

THE BASIC FOUNDATION

At some point during the boatbuilding process, the realization will strike—you're going to need a sail soon. Basically you have two choices: You can either design and build the sail yourself, or have a loft do that for you. In either case you will need to educate yourself with as much information as possible to ensure that the sail will match both your needs and those of the boat.

A quick flip through any design catalog will reveal a wide variety of sailing rigs. Each one of those rigs has requirements that need to be met for the sails and boat to perform at maximum. If you are building a sharpie, a Swampscott Dory, or any number of traditional boats, the odds are that the plans won't show it as a masthead sloop. Even many of the "modern" stitch-and-glue designs are being drawn with traditional sails rather than a Bermudian main and jib.

However, most production boats have a Bermudian sail, and that is what the majority of sail makers are familiar with. And most of the literature on sail making describes making the ubiquitous Bermudian sail. So how does the builder resolve this problem?

A brief review of how a sail works and some of the language of sail making is a good place to start. For a sail to move a boat to the windward, it needs a curved surface pointed into the wind at the proper angle. The curved surface changes the way air flows across the surface of the sail, thus creating drive. This is very basic information that every sailor understands. And there have been several books written that examine, in great detail, the physics involved in sailing. *Aero-Hydrodynamics of Sailing* by C. A. Marchaj (International Marine Publishing, Camden, Maine) is one of many volumes on the subject that will provide builders with highly technical information. It is good to remember, however, that sailors have been designing and building sails for several thousand years with no more information than that a curved surface moves a boat to the windward.

The degree and shape of the curved surface has a direct relationship to how efficiently the sail functions. It also affects the range of conditions, such as wind velocity and amount of chop, where the sail will operate best.

To help visualize and design the shape of

the sail, imagine several straight lines drawn across a sail from luff to leech (**Figure 1-01**). Those hypothetical lines are chords forming the baseline for the draft or curve of the sail. The amount of draft or

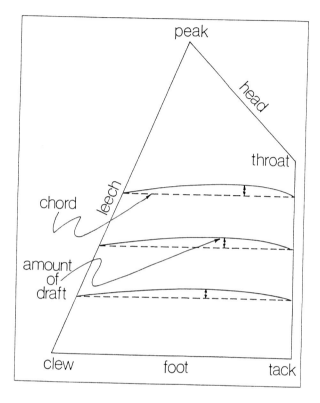

Figure 1-01

curve for a given sail can be flatter or fuller, depending on the range of conditions in which the boat normally sails. A flatter sail can point higher than the same sail with more draft, and can also be faster under some conditions. The downside is that it has a narrower angle that the sail will draw at its full potential. In other words, the helmsman will have to pay more attention to the angle of attack; put another way, the less draft a sail has, the smaller its window of maximum performance.

The same sail with more draft designed into its shape doesn't need as much attention to the helm and will have more power to move the boat into a chop. Too much draft, however, causes a progression of problems. A sail with a large draft will not point as high as its flatter counterpart, and adding even more draft causes the sail to lose driving power. So there is a point of diminishing returns at each end of the draft continuum.

The amount of draft is generally expressed in a ratio such as 1:10 or 1:13: that is 1 foot of draft for 10 feet of chord or 1 foot of draft for 13 feet of chord. Sails with ratios that range from 1:10 to 1:13 fall in the average amount of draft, with 1:10 being toward the full end and 1:13 toward the flat end. Ratios of 1:7 and 1:20 represent the extreme ends for sails.

Not only is the depth of the draft important, but where the greatest draft falls along the chord also affects the sail's performance; too far forward or too far aft and performance suffers. Sails that have the maximum draft at a point 35 to 50 percent aft of the luff are average. The sail in **Figure 1-02** has the maximum draft at a point that is 45 percent of the chord aft of the luff for each chord. Marchaj in *Sailing Theory and Practice* (Dodd, Mead and Company, New York) found that a sail with the maximum draft at 50 percent of the chord from the luff was best for sailing on the wind, and sails

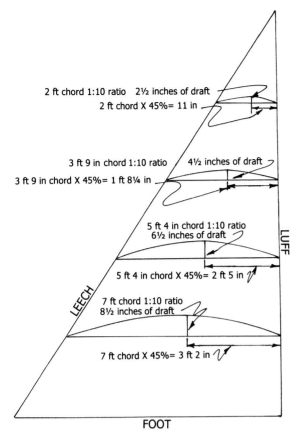

2 ft chord 1:10 ratio   2½ inches of draft
2 ft chord X 45%= 11 in

3 ft 9 in chord 1:10 ratio   4½ inches of draft
3 ft 9 in chord X 45%= 1 ft 8¼ in

5 ft 4 in chord 1:10 ratio
6½ inches of draft

5 ft 4 in chord X 45%= 2 ft 5 in

7 ft chord 1:10 ratio
8½ inches of draft

7 ft chord X 45%= 3 ft 2 in

LUFF

LEECH

FOOT

Figure 1-02

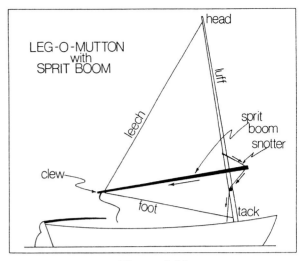

LEG-O-MUTTON
with
SPRIT BOOM

head

luff

sprit
boom
snotter

leech

clew

foot

tack

Figure 1-03

with the maximum draft greater than 50 percent were best on a reach. He also found that greater wind speed moved the maximum draft point more forward. It should be remembered, however, that these figures represent a Bermudian sail with a jib, and what works for one type of sail doesn't necessarily work for all types of sails.

A good example of this is an 18-foot sharpie with two types of sailing rigs—a Bermudian sail with a jib and a leg-of-mutton with a sprit boom. The sharpie with its flat bottom is an easily driven hull. In most cases, an easily driven hull will have a sail with a relatively small amount of draft; that's the way most sail makers would build

a Bermudian sail for this hull. The leg-of-mutton sail (**Figure 1-03**) is an entirely different story, even though both sails are the same basic triangular shape. Because of the characteristics of the sprit boom, it is possible to build much more draft into the sail. Also, the draft placement should be closer to the luff than in the Bermudian sail. This allows the sail to function in a wider range of conditions. As the wind speed increases the snotter can be tightened, forcing the sprit and clew out and flattening the sail. As the winds decrease the snotter can be eased, putting more shape and power into the sail. If the sail maker or designer doesn't know this, the owner of the latter sharpie will wind up with a flattish sail, thereby losing much of the rig's potential.

Other examples are the Chinese lug sail and the gaff sail. Both sails have the same general trapezoidal shape but each sail uses a different method to give the sail shape or draft.

The panels of the Chinese lug sail are sewn together straight edge to straight edge and battens give the sail its shape. The gaff sail in **Figure 1-04** uses broadseaming, a technique that cuts small wedges or pies from the side of the panels to give the sail shape along the luff and head.

While battens and broadseaming give shape to the sail, the type of sailcloth also affects sail shape and how long a sail will last. Dacron tends to be used more than cotton or other synthetics such as nylon. It's more ultraviolet (UV) resistant than

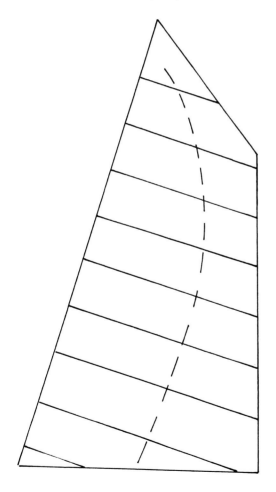

Figure 1-04

either cotton or nylon, and its strength-to-weight ratio is very good. Also, cotton and nylon are more susceptible to mildew. However, in *Skiffs and Schooners* (International Marine/McGraw Hill Books, Camden, Maine), R. D. Culler makes a strong case for cotton treated with Cuprinol. He claims it lasts as long as any man-made fiber. Certainly it would be hard to find a more traditional material, but most builders will find Dacron's shape holding characteristics and other qualities are better suited to their needs.

Another factor that determines sail shape is how the cloth stretches when it's under load. Cloth can be woven so its main strength is along its length or its width, or it can be equally strong in both directions. Warp-oriented cloth has the main strength along its length; fill-oriented cloth is strongest across the width. Sailcloth also stretches diagonally, or at a 45-degree angle to the length. This bias stretch is controlled by adding fillers to the spaces between the threads in a process called calenderizing. Calenderizing, however, does make the cloth stiffer and somewhat harder to handle.

Choosing a warp- or fill-oriented cloth will depend on how the sail is cut. If the panels are parallel to the leech, the sail is sail to be cut vertically; a crosscut sail has the panels at a 90-degree angle to the leech (**Figure 1-05**). On traditional sails that are cut vertically, the greatest stress or loading

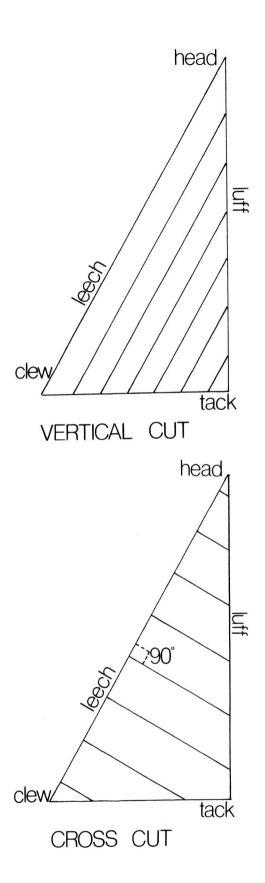

VERTICAL CUT

CROSS CUT

Figure 1-05

is along the leech from the clew to the head or peak. A warp-oriented cloth is appropriate for this cut, but with small sails a balanced cloth could be used as well. Fill-oriented cloth is the best choice for sails that are crosscut, as the wind stresses the cloth most at its width. A balanced cloth can be used for small crosscut sails rather than fill-oriented cloth, as well.

Wind is not the only stress factor with traditional sails. Rigging also creates loading in some areas of the sail. Both standing lug sails and balanced lug sails use a downhaul to keep the luff tight and improve windward performance. The use of the downhaul makes the reinforcement of the luff very important for the sail's longevity.

There are some leg-of-mutton sails that also use a downhaul, requiring that the luff be strengthened. That same leg-of-mutton sail with a sprit boom will need to have the foot reinforced, because one of the main stress areas on this sail is from tack to clew. Also, many designers familiar with traditional sails feel the foot should have little or no roach—that is, the foot should be cut straight. If the foot is given a large roach and not reinforced, the sail will not perform as well and will have a shorter life.

Another factor that affects the overall performance of the sail and boat is the weight of the sailcloth. Some plans suggest the cut and cloth weight of the sail, as well as sail area. However, there is some room for change to get a sail and rig exactly suited to the builder. If there is a cloth weight indicated on the plans, it may still be possible to use a lighter weight of cloth. This will be particularly true if the plans are from the 1950s or earlier. Sailcloth's weight-to-strength ratio has improved over the years, and most small boats shouldn't need cloth heavier than 3.9 to 4.5 ounces per yard. Remember that heavy cloth aloft just adds to the heeling moment, and just like the draft continuum, there are losses when the cloth is too light or too heavy.

Even if there is no cloth weight suggested, there may be more than one rig type shown as an option. It is in the builder's best interest to know the strong and weak points of the suggested rigs. Knowing which rig your sail maker is most familiar with is reason enough to choose one sail over another. Even if there are no alternatives listed, it's possible to change from a standing lug to a balanced lug or a leg-of-mutton to a sliding gunter without appreciably altering the center of effort or lead. Making these changes requires a good understanding of the rigs and your own needs.

Another alteration that can be made without effect on performance is changing from a vertical to crosscut or vice versa, but panel width will have a direct effect on sail shape. The fewer the panels, the fewer opportunities you or the sail maker will have to put in shape with broadseaming; too many panels, however, and the sail becomes far more labor-intensive.

While the plans may indicate the cut of the sail, they may not show other details such as lacing. If it does suggest one type, it most likely won't show more than one method, and there are several ways to lace a sail to the mast or yard. Not only are there variations in lacing, but robands and wooden hoops are also options. One of the best features about traditional sails is all the possibilities the builder has when rigging the boat and designing the sail. Making a decision about what option is best before the builder starts will help ensure a sail that is matched to the boat and owner.

2

THE MARLINSPIKE KIT— A SAILOR'S AND WATERMAN'S FRIEND

In the not-too-distant past, sailors and watermen alike repaired broken gear and made new equipment for their boats. Sailors patched torn sails, made bull's-eyes, and spliced running rigging while the waterman leathered oars, spliced dock lines, and created tie-downs for cargo. Both did an endless number of jobs and created an amazing variety of gear, all with the small and simple marlinspike kit. Yet most modern sailors and boatmen would be hard pressed to describe its contents,

much less have one on board. The need hasn't vanished from boats, just the kit. And by ignoring this tried-and-true friend, boat owners and boatbuilders bind themselves to boatyards and chandleries.

There is nothing complicated or expensive in a marlinspike kit, so it's hard to understand why this has happened. Spill the contents of a typical kit on the deck and there's nothing arcane or difficult to find. **Figure 2-01** shows a sail maker's palm (there is also a left-handed model), a knife, a wooden fid, a steel awl, a steel marlinspike, whipping thread, and an assortment of sail-making needles in a small container. Other tools can be added, of course, but with this simple kit the builder or owner can make almost anything needed for the boat from rope and wood.

There two choices when it comes to buying a palm: a roping palm and a seam-

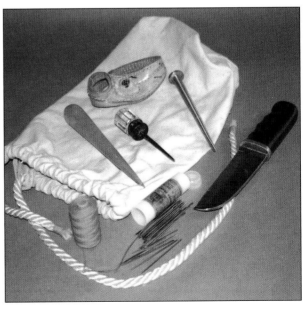

Figure 2-01

ing palm. The roping palm has a hard ear over the thumb to help haul whipping thread tight as well as an eye to push the needle through canvas and sailcloth. **Figure 2-02** shows a roping palm with whipping

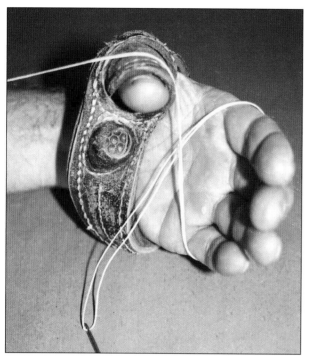

Figure 2-02

thread over the ear ready to haul tight. The seaming palm in **Figure 2-01** is missing the hard ear and is designed to just push the needle through cloth. Most boat owners will find the hauling ear of the roping palm a real benefit when whipping the ends of rope (to the purist, and those who insist on being technically correct, a rope becomes a line when it comes on board a boat) or serving a splice.

Because the palm is central to the marlinspike kit, it is essential to own a good one. Nothing will discourage marlinspike

work like a poorly made and poorly fitting palm. Sail makers go to great lengths to make sure the palm fits their hand. Some recommend soaking the palm in warm water and then letting it dry on the hand. Once dry, it should be well oiled and cleaned. While the average boat owner may not go to such lengths, a well-fitting palm is critical. If it is heavily made with rawhide leather and well stitched together, it will give years of service, allowing it to be passed on to the young sailor or waterman.

The fid is as indispensable as the roping palm for splicing and other marlinspike work. The wooden fid in **Figure 2-01** was made by the author from rock maple, but a fid may be made from steel or plastic as well. There are also several fid variations on the market and all will do the job of parting the strands of a line, allowing another strand to be passed through. However, trying to make an eye splice or knock a thimble into a cringle without a fid will test the patience of the most calm.

Any fid—wood, metal, or plastic— should not have a very sharp point. A sharp point will catch the individual fibers of the line, pulling them out and generally causing problems. However, a fid with too blunt a point will not separate the strands of the line, particularly smaller sizes. Rounding the point in small degrees will be the most useful course of action and keep from ruining a good fid.

The awl in **Figure 2-01** is more useful in splicing small-diameter rope than the larger fid. And like the fid, the awl's point shouldn't be too sharp. Some experimenting will help determine just the right point shape, and a little time spent finding the right point for both tools at the start will pay dividends later.

While the awl excels at splicing small line, it also does double duty as a leather punch. A light tap with the fid or hammer punches a hole in canvas, sailcloth, or leather, allowing a needle to be pushed through with a minimum of effort. When leathering a pair of oars, an awl is almost essential for a neat and seaman-like job. This use as a punch should be considered when shaping the point.

What is true for the points of the fid and awl is also true for the sail-making needles. It does seem strange that needles shouldn't have a sharp point, but rounding the point slightly will help stop the needle from catching on the fibers of the line or cloth. A whetstone will work best for rounding and dulling the points and the edges. Because of the triangular shape of the sail making needles, the edges should also be rounded over slightly if they are sharp.

Sail-making needles come in different sizes, with the smaller numbers being the larger needles. An 18, 16, or 14 needle will do most of the work, but it's good to have various sizes and several of each. An assortment of needles can be found at many marine suppliers, with the needles manufactured by Wm. Smith and Co. generally considered the best.

While needles, fids, and awls should be dulled slightly, the knife in a marlinspike kit should be very sharp. The knife in **Figure 2-01** was patterned after the design in Hervey Garrett Smith's *The Arts of the Sailor* (John De Graff, Inc., Tuckahoe, New York) and custom-made for the author. The spine of the knife is wide and heavy so it can be struck with a mallet or a heavy fid to cut a line. If the knife is sharp, a crisp, clean cut will be the result. It is possible to cut a line in this manner and not have the blade scar the surface underneath. However, cutting a line on a teak deck or varnished mahogany rail is definitely not for the weakhearted; a scrap board is highly recommended under the cut.

It isn't necessary to have a custom-made knife to cut a rope. Almost any strong blade will do. A Swiss Army knife with some of the heavier blades will work nicely, and the knives in the Multi-Plier Pocket Tool by Gerber slice through a piece of line very well. Both have the added benefit of extra tools. It should be noted that neither blade will survive a heavy blow with a mallet, so a light hand should be used on both.

The last item in the basic marlinspike kit, the twine, is the glue that holds much of the marlinspike work together. To increase the longevity of the work, it must be not only strong but also UV resistant and right for the specific task. There are several different types of twine, and some twine comes in different weights. All are Dacron, which makes them all resistant to UV light, but each twine has slightly varying characteristics that make some better for certain tasks.

Probably the most useful to most boat owners will be twine that is twisted. The primary function of this twine is for whipping and seizing line. It comes in white and light brown. The brown color looks very nice when used on white three-strand rope, particularly if some fancy needle work has been done.

Certainly twisted line could be used to sew a bronze ring to a sail or even sew on a patch (white would be the color of choice here), but these tasks are better suited to a round, lightly waxed twine. This twine's shape seems to work better with sewn rings and brass liners as well as patches on sails. This maybe a matter of personal preference as much as anything else, but the round twine doesn't work quite as well for whipping the ends of line.

There is also a heavily waxed, flat thread that is best for sewing bronze rings to sailcloth. Some might find it good for whipping the ends of line but the wax always winds up looking dirty. The heavy wax does give the twine better protection from the elements,

but in most cases the trade-off isn't worth the aesthetic cost of the extra dirt.

There is one more type of twine, but the average boat owner will have not have much need for it in his or her kit. Tarred marline was as common as a marlinspike on ships and boats before synthetic cordage, but nylon and Dacron have made it a relic of the past. It is still available and it does some tasks better than all others, but the pine tar gets on white sails and decks, not to mention clothes, making it very unpopular.

To discuss tarred marline and not mention its very distinctive smell would be a gross oversight. There are some who find it an unpleasant odor. Others find it a pleasing fragrance that evokes visions of hemp line and real canvas sails. Whatever the opinion, almost all agree it is, in fact, distinctive. If the marlinspike kit is kept on board in a locker (and it should be), the tarred marline will drive out all musty, mildew odors on the boat.

While tarred marline would have been a part of any traditional marlinspike kit of the past, there is one tool that wasn't around during the days of hemp and pine tar: the Fid-O. This handy tool can make the splicing of three-strand line much easier. The directions that come with the tool are easy to understand, and it's not expensive. (See www.fid-o.com.)

The most complete marlinspike kit on the water won't do the boat owner a bit of good without the knowledge and skills to put it to use. The most basic skills involve knowing how to whip the end of a line, seizing (that is, securing a loop, eye, or thimble in line by wrapping it with twine), and making an eye splice. None takes a great deal of time to master, yet the amount of gear that can be fashioned from these three simple skills is astounding.

The first skill, whipping, stops line from fraying or unwrapping. There are several ways to keep rope from fraying, but the most attractive, whipping, is also the longest lasting. The butane melt and the tape wrap both work, but that is all that can be said in their favor. Yet a properly done whipping should last the useful life of the line and add to the seaman-like appearance of the boat.

A "common whipping" can be done without a palm and needle, which makes it a little faster to do. **Figure 2-03** shows a

loop laid out toward the end of the line with the twine crossing over and continuing with very tight wraps over the loop. The wraps should extend up about the diameter of the line; then the working end is passed through the loop. Pull the end of the loop slowly, taking out any slack. When all the slack is out, pull the working end under the wraps with an easy jerk. This brings both ends of the twine under the wraps and keeps them from unraveling.

While the common whipping is slightly faster, it is not as long lasting as the "palm-and-needle whipping" and should be considered only temporary. On the other hand, the palm-and-needle buries the twine in the line, wraps over the bury, and uses diagonal turns to keep the wraps tight. This makes it a sturdy and able job. In **Figure 2-04a**, a doubled piece of twine is passed back and forth through the line, stitching away from the end. On the last

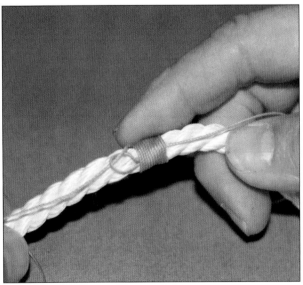

Figure 2-03

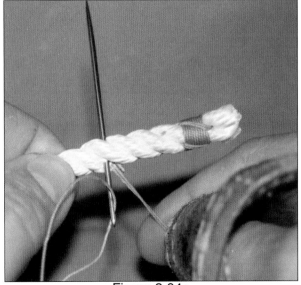

Figure 2-04a

stitch, the twine should come out between strands as shown. Then, working against the lay of the line (in other words, against the direction the line is twisted), a number of very tight wraps are put on toward the end. This is where the ear on the roping palm will serve well to haul the wraps tight. It's important to keep all the twists out of the twine because twists will stand up and chafe, spoiling the neat appearance of the whipping.

When a sufficient number of wraps have been put on (this will be about equal to the line diameter), find where the twine started the wraps and follow that groove up to the top of the wraps, shown **Figure 2-04b**.

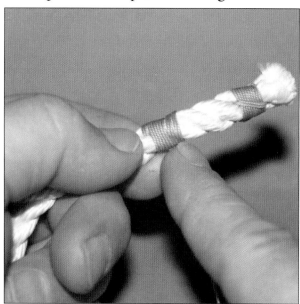

Figure 2-04b

This is where the needle should end the wraps, bringing the twine out on the other side of the strand, **Figure 2-04c**. Notice that the end of the line is now turned in the opposite direction, and that the needle ended the

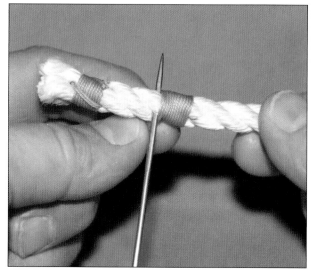

Figure 2-04c

wrapping turns on the line but in the opposite direction of the wrapping turns. Bring the twine down the line between the strands and push the needle under and out into the next line between strands as in **Figure 2-04d**. Repeat the procedure bringing the twine up between strands and passing the needle under one side of the strand and out the other, **Figure 2-04e**. The twine should now be where the wrapping turns ended.

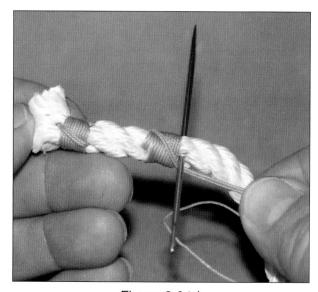

Figure 2-04d

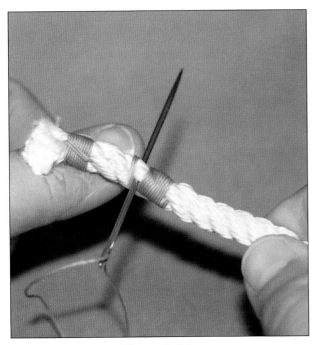

Figure 2-04e

Before the last diagonal turn is made, it's very important to bring the needle under and over the top wrap so that the twine will pull it down tight against the rest of the turns, **Figure 2-04f**. The twine is brought down between the strands and ended as

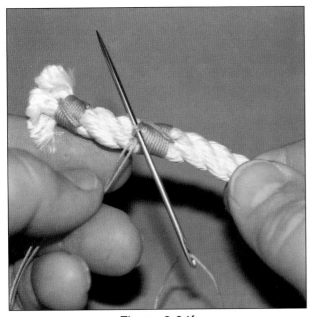

Figure 2-04f

before. Here the needle is pushed under where the first wrapping turn started, **Figure 2-04g**. This will pull the turn tight against the body of the whipping.

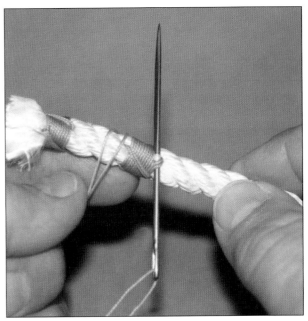

Figure 2-04g

Figure 2-04h

To finish the whipping, pass the needle under the diagonal turn to create a knot, pull it down, bury the twine in the line, and cut the twine flush. If the line is to see very heavy use, a second needle-and-palm whipping is highly recommended three or four rope diameters down from the first. This provides a backup should the first whipping fail (**Figure 2-04h**).

There are a number of variations on the needle-and-palm whipping. *The Marlinspike Sailor* by Hervey Garrett Smith (John De Graff, Inc.) details a "snaked whipping"; there are others, like the "West County whipping" that do not use a needle and palm. Still, the method shown above, detailed by Brion Toss in his book *The Rigger's Apprentice* (International Marine/ McGraw-Hill Book), is easy to learn and fast to do. While this may not be the only way to whip the end of a line with a needle and palm, it is important for the owner to find a method that works and then tenaciously stick to that method.

Unlike the whipping that uses a doubled length of twine, seizing an eye in a rope uses a single piece of twine with a loop or eye in the end. Certainly the easiest way to make this loop is to twist the twine against the lay and tuck the end through the twine two or three times, **Figure 2-05a**. For a truly stout loop, leave a tail for the wrapping turns to pass over, as in **Figure 2-05b**.

The next step is to apply the appropriate number of wrapping turns. These turns should be applied very tight, and make sure about every third turn is very, very tight. There is no hard-and-fast rule for the

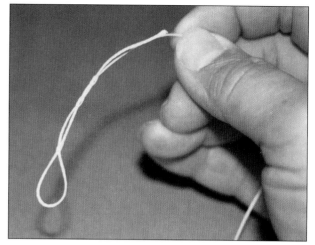
Figure 2-05a

Figure 2-05b

number of turns, but a little more than the combined width of the two lines seems to look good and have adequate strength. If the seizing will take a great deal of wear or chafe, then a second set of riding turns might be called for.

A riding turn is nothing more than a second set of turns that ride up and over the first wrapping turns. The trick is to pass the first riding turn under the last wrapping turn (**Figure 2-05c**) and then carefully put the riding turns in the groove between each wrapping turn as the twine is brought back down and over the first layer.

Figure 2-05c

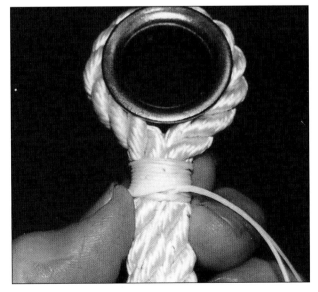

Figure 2-05d

The riding turns are finished by threading the twine through the loop (**Figure 2-05d**) and then up and over for two or three rounding turns, **Figure 2-05e**. To finish off seizing the thimble or eye, pass the twine under the rounding turns and knot off (**Figures 2-05f** and **2-05g**).

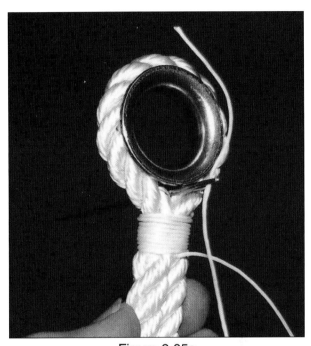

Figure 2-05e

Figure 2-05f

Figure 2-05g

Figure 2-05h

There is nothing difficult about seizing; having this ability allows the creation of so much gear for the boat, yet most boat owners don't possess the skill. Even fewer know how to make an eye splice, but the eye splice is no more difficult than the seized eye. It takes a bit of practice and a small investment in time, but it's time well spent.

It will be best to start with some practice rope that has a somewhat hard lay. Dacron or polyester three-strand rope seems to be better to learn with because it has a harder lay or is stiffer than nylon three-strand. The harder lay keeps the strands separated and makes handling the line an easier task. Manila rope also has a hard lay; it can be found in any hardware store and is much less expensive than Dacron. Some will find this a better practice rope, but 15 or 20 feet of 3/8" Dacron or polyester rope costs only a few cents more a foot and the successes can be used on the boat.

Start with a section of rope, either Dacron or manila, about 30 inches in length, with one end temporarily wrapped with masking tape. Put a needle-and-palm whipping approximately 6 to 8 inches from the untaped end, and then after wrapping the end of each strand with tape, unlay each strand back to the whipping. The tape keeps the working strand from unraveling, and twisting the tape to a point makes it easier to push the working strands through the rope. An eye with a diameter of about 3 inches will be easy to handle, so bring the whipping around to create a loop that size, use the fid or marlinspike to make an opening under a strand, and pull #1 (red) under that strand as shown in **Figure 2-06a**. Then pass #2 (yellow) *over* the strand that #1 went under and pull it *under* the next strand (**Figure 2-06b**). In the next

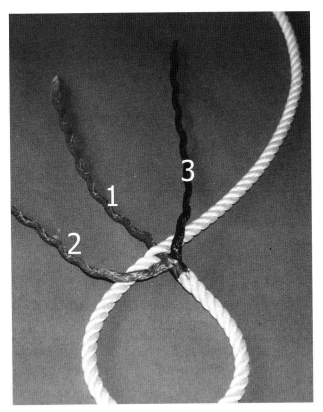

Figure 2-06a

Figure 2-06b

Figure 2-06c

Figure 2-06d

Figure 2-06e

Figure 2-06f

step the eye is turned over or capsized. This puts the whipping on the left and exposes the strand between #2 and #1. The tip of the fid points to this strand in **Figure 2-06c**. Pass #3 (black) *under* that strand, pulling it back to the left as shown in **Figure 2-06d**. Turn the loop back over so the whipping is on the right side once more; starting with #2, go over one strand and under the next. This is followed by #1 and #3 in that order (**Figure 2-06e**). About five sets of tucks will make the splice secure, even in ropes with a soft lay (**Figure 2-06f**).

At this juncture there are several ways to finish out the splice. The working ends can be left to wear away, but a more aesthetically pleasing splice can be made by a palm-and-needle whipping over the working strands.

There is no reason that a perfectly acceptable eye splice can't be made on the first try. However, it will be best to use the remaining rope to make more. The more practice, the more familiar the skill will become—and there will always be uses for those short pieces of line with an eye splice.

There are any number of books written on the subject of marlinspike skills, but *The Marlinspike Sailor* by Harvey Garrett Smith is about the best place to start for a great deal of the information. This classic has not only clear and easy-to-understand instructions, but also some extremely useful projects for any boat. *The Arts of the Sailor*, by Smith as well, has some truly great applications of marlinspike skills that will dress up any boat.

It's good to remember that it's not necessary to read volumes of books and spend a year or two before the mast to learn a few basic marlinspike skills. Yet investing the time to learn how to whip the end of a rope, seize an eye, and make an eye splice enables the boat owner to create an astounding amount of gear to make the operation of the boat easier and improve its appearance.

3

REPLACING A MODERN SAILING RIG WITH A TRADITIONAL ONE

One hundred years ago, when a boat owner chose a boat design, the odds were very good that it included some sort of traditional sail. At the turn of the century and earlier, the Bermudian sail or Marconi sail was not very popular. Today a large number of sailboats are designed with a Bermuda rig even when it might not be the best choice. Also, when a traditional sail is shown on the design, it may not be the sail the builder wants. As a result, prospective builders may find a limited number of designs that meet their needs. Nevertheless, it is possible to find a good hull design and then retrofit a sail plan that is more to the owner's liking.

To accomplish the retrofitting process, the builder needs only a basic understanding of the factors that determined the placement of the original sailing rig, and why that placement created what is called a "balanced rig."

In the most simple terms, balance occurs when two points—the center of lateral resistance (CLR) of the boat and the center of effort (COE) of the sail plan—interact in a manner that keeps the boat moving forward without rounding up into the wind (weather helm) or falling off downwind (lee helm). **Figure 3-01** shows a typical location of both points. In most cases the boat will balance better if the center of effort of the sail is in front of, or "leads," the center of lateral

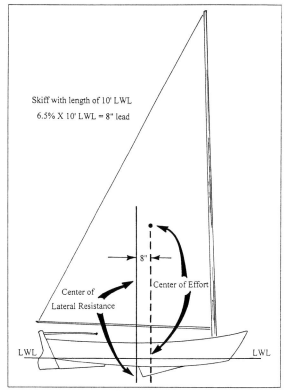

Skiff with length of 10' LWL
6.5% X 10' LWL = 8" lead

8"

Center of Effort

Center of Lateral Resistance

LWL

LWL

Figure 3-01

resistance. The boat in **Figure 3-01** has a 6.5 percent lead (6.5 percent of the waterline length), but the exact amount of lead varies from design to design. Most designs seem to have a 5 to 10 percent lead.

Having the COE in front of the CLR is necessary because as the boat heels over, the footprint or the waterline of the boat becomes asymmetrical. This causes the boat to round up into the wind (weather helm). Imagine the symmetrical bullet-shaped waterline of the upright hull; as the boat heels over and starts to move forward, this bullet shape becomes a curved U shape, and this asymmetrical U shape causes the boat to round up into the wind. Moving the COE of the sail in front of the CLR helps to counterbalance this asymmetry of the hull.

When retrofitting with a traditional sail, or changing one traditional sail for another, the builder must not change the existing amount of lead for the design. To keep from disturbing this balance, the traditional sail's COE must match the COE of the sail it's replacing. This is not as difficult as it might seem, assuming the builder is working from a set of plans that has a sail plan. The sail plan will show where the COE is for the existing sail and where it is in relationship to the hull. The builder only needs to know the COE for the traditional sail and superimpose it to determine where the new sail and mast will fall.

Figure 3-02 shows the sail plan for a 14

foot skiff. It has the dimension of the main sail and jib, the height, rake, and location of the mast, and the combined COE for both sails. If the sail plan doesn't show the COE, it can be easily calculated.

Figure 3-03 is a triangular main and jib, drawn to scale. The same scale as the sail plan should be used; if the plans are in a book, any convenient scale can be used. A

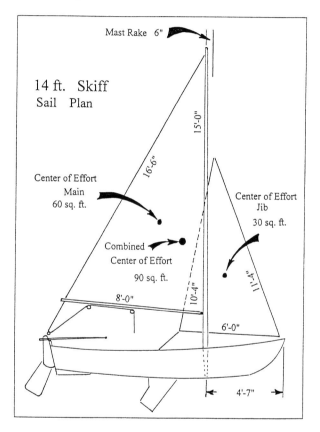

Figure 3-02

line is drawn from the midpoint of one side (A) to the opposite apex (B). Then do this for all sides. The resulting intersection of lines at C and D is the theoretical or geometrical center of effort for each sail.

The combined COE of both sails is

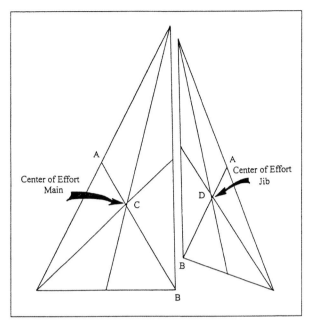

Figure 3-03

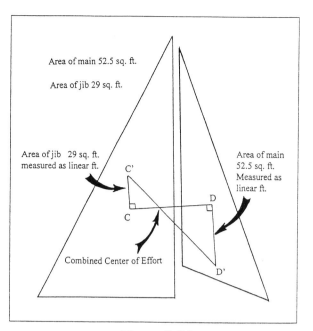

Figure 3-04

found by first connecting the individual COEs (points C and D in **Figure 3-04**). Then, at right angles to C and D, draw lines in opposite directions. For the next step, the area of both sails must be known. This will probably be on the sail plan but if not, calculate the areas using standard formulas. Once this data is at hand, transfer the area of the main sail into linear feet on line D/D'. A small scale should be used—3/32 inch equals 1 foot or smaller. Next, the area of the jib is transferred to line C/C'. Connecting points C' and D' will give the combined center of effort for both sails.

Once this has been established, it will be necessary to do the same for the traditional sail. However, before moving on to this step, some important questions should be answered. The primary question should be: Is the existing sail too large or too small?

This is the time to make adjustments. If other boats of similar type, size, and weight have about the same sail area, then the area is probably correct. If not, then an adjustment might be in order. The table in **Figure 3-05** was compiled from a book written by E. C. Seibert, *How to Design Small Boats* (Dodd, Mead and Company, New York). According to the table in this 1947 book, a 14-foot, unballasted shoal draft boat carrying 95 square feet would be on the small side, while 200 square feet would be on the large side and 160 would be average. It should be noted that the sail areas that Mr. Seibert considered to be on the small side are, by today's standards, more the norm. The skiff in **Figure 3-02** has a 90-square-foot sail, and the builder might want to adjust the area slightly up or down to suit the prevailing winds where the boat will be

Sail Area of Unballasted Sailboat

	11 feet	12 feet	13 feet	14 feet	15 feet	16 feet
HIGH	104 SQ FT	128 SQ FT	160 SQ FT	200 SQ FT	250 SQ FT	300 SQ FT
MED	90 SQ FT	98 SQ FT	130 SQ FT	160 SQ FT	195 SQ FT	225 SQ FT
LOW	62 SQ FT	72 SQ FT	83 SQ FT	**95 SQ FT**	105 SQ FT	115 SQ FT

Figure 3-05

sailed. If the design is well tested, you can assume the sail area is correct and avoid any large changes in either direction.

Having settled on the sail area, the next question should be: To jib or not to jib? The existing sail plan might call for a jib, but that doesn't necessarily mean the traditionally rigged boat must have one. One of the joys of traditional sails is their simplicity. Stepping an unstayed mast and dealing with a single halyard and no boom are a few of the advantages of boats with traditional sails. In many cases, the advantages of better laminar flow created by the jib and the fast reduction in sail area by dropping it are offset by more halyards, sheets, standing rigging, and one more sail to deal with on a tack. If the builder decides that "less is more," then designing the replacement will be even simpler.

When designing the traditional sail, here are a few things to keep in mind: The foot shouldn't be so long that the cleating point for the mainsheet will be aft of the transom, and the clew should be high enough to allow reasonable visibility. This may require some trial-and-error design work to establish the right combination. However, paper is cheap and work done on the drawing board will help eliminate more expensive problems down the road.

Also, finding the center of effort for a four-sided sail is different from a triangular sail, but there are at least three methods that can be used. Perhaps the simplest is related to the method for finding the combined center of effort. In **Figure 3-06**, a line is drawn from the throat to the clew. This divides the sail into two triangles. The geometric center of these two triangles is found by using the method found in **Figure 3-02**. Having established the two centers (CE1 and CE2), connect them with a line. Then draw the perpendicular lines as in **Figure 3-04** and scale off the areas of each triangle along CE1' and CE2'. Connecting the resulting points will give the center of effort

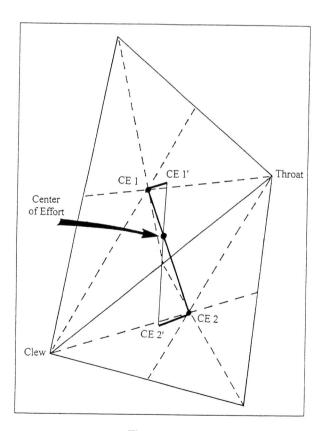

Figure 3-06

for the trapezoidal sail.

The center of effort of the traditional sail is now placed directly over the combined center of effort of the original sail plan. This gives the builder a location for the new mast that will not change the original lead or the balance of the boat. Because all of these calculations are estimates of points that will be in a constant state of flux while the boat is under sail, it's best to consider this location a starting point to be fine-tuned after launching.

This method will allow the builder to change out one main sail for another, but won't help the builder who wants to add a mizzen where there is none. There are many advantages to having a mizzen, including control on all points of sail. Sheeting in a mizzen hard or sailing with it eased will help balance the helm. **Figure 3-07** shows an 18-foot sharpie with Bermudian sail and jib and the center of effort for the sail plan. **Figure 3-08** shows the same sharpie with a shoulder-of-mutton main and a leg-of-mutton mizzen, and the combined center of effort for both sails. The old sail plan and COE are shown as dotted lines. It may take several attempts to find the right spacing of the main and mizzen so that COE matches the original COE. Just as when changing one main sail for another, it is very wise to consider the placement of the main and mizzen as starting points.

Some adjustability at the mast partner is always a good idea. This will allow the rake

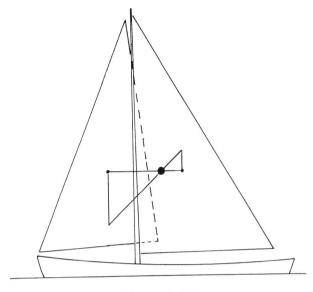

Figure 3-07

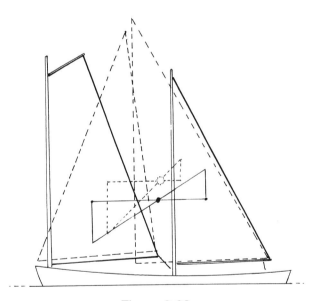

Figure 3-08

of the mast and the center of effort of the sail to be moved fore and aft as needed. Once on the water, if the boat is found to have too much weather helm, the rake of the mast can be decreased. This will move the center of effort forward and increase the lead. Adding a jib, increasing its size, or moving it forward are just a few of the more drastic methods to increase the lead and decrease the weather helm.

Load placement is another factor that should be considered before making drastic changes to the sail plan. Load placement will definitely change the balance of a small boat. Watching a St. Lawrence River Skiff tack through a race course just by shifting the weight of the crew fore and aft is convincing evidence of the enormous effect of load placement. This is also a simple means of keeping the boat in balance.

Lee helm, something to be avoided, can be eliminated by moving the center of effort aft or decreasing the lead. Increasing the rake of the mast will be the simplest means of moving the center of effort aft and decreasing the lead. Decreasing the size of the jib or removing it altogether will also move the center of effort aft and shorten the amount of lead, which will in turn eliminate the unwanted lee helm. If this is not enough, then stepping the mast farther aft might be the next remedy. However, it's a good idea to remember that correcting lee helm or increasing weather helm may be as simple as moving the weight of the crew forward. This should be tried before embarking on more drastic measures.

Finding the balance for a sailboat is really a compromise of various factors that are in a constant state of change, and allowing for some adjustment once the boat is launched

is very important. If this is done, then the process will be a satisfying and successful change. Even adding a mizzen won't create balance problems and will add to the enjoyment of the boat.

Should all this seem like too much work to have a traditional sail like a standing lug or sprit sail, there is always the sliding gunter rig. The center of effort of the sliding gunter, basically a triangular sail, will match almost exactly the center of effort for the Bermuda sail, yet the mast and spar will fit inside the boat. The use of the sliding gunter will eliminate all of the above work to match the lead of the existing sail plan, and will also use the same mast step. Again, it would be advisable to allow for some adjustment at the mast partner.

Builders of small boats shouldn't be intimidated by rig design. Feel free to experiment and examine your alternatives. The use of scale drawings will allow experimenting with multiple rigs and help make the decision about the sail that best meets the builder's requirements. Retrofitting a boat with a traditional sail is easily done, and with a traditional hull type, will probably result in a more aesthetically pleasing, easier-handling boat.

4

THE SLIDING GUNTER— A VERSATILE TRADITIONAL SAILING RIG

The sliding gunter is a traditional rig that has always been more popular in Europe than on this side of the Atlantic, but it's hard to find a better sailing rig for small boats. One of the main advantages of the gunter is the use of a mast and vertical spar to achieve the same mast height and sail area as the Bermuda rig would set. This means the unstepped mast and all the spars can fit inside the boat when under oar power or traveling on a trailer.

Many whaleboats—a real study in efficiency—used the sliding gunter, particularly in the Azores. The whalers found that a long mast hanging over the end of the boat was not an asset when attached to several tons of a very angry whale. Also, stepping and unstepping a shorter mast was easier and faster for the whalers—and that, of course, applies to the recreational boater as well. Yet all this convenience and ease comes in the same size and shape as the Bermuda sail.

The sail is convenient, but is it fast? Yes, according to Jeremy Howard-Williams in *Small Boat Sails* (International Marine, Camden, Maine). He found that wind tunnel tests showed the gunter was as fast on the wind as the Bermuda and actually faster off the wind. Also, C. A. Marchaj in *Sailing Theory and Practice* gives the gunter very high marks for aerodynamic shape and lower induced drag. According to Marchaj, the gunter achieves the same effect as the Bermuda with a bending mast. But the gunter does it without all the high-tech gear that comes with a bending-mast Bermuda. This allows the gunter sailor to get high-tech results with low-tech gear.

Detractors of the gunter rig are quick to point out that the yard falls off from the mast on a beat to the wind, creating turbulent airflow, and is therefore slower than the Bermudian sail. The debate on this can be complicated, with both sides quoting data to make each case. Perhaps the main question the builder must ask is: Do the advantages outweigh the disadvantages?

And an understanding that choosing any sailing rig is always giving up an advantage to gain another.

One of the main advantages of the gunter rig doesn't become obvious until the sail is reefed. Then the spar comes down as well and brings its weight with it. The photos in **Figures 4-01a** and **4-01b** illustrate how this not only maintains a low center of effort for the sail, but also eliminates the extra weight of the mast aloft. This has a very positive effect on a boat in strong winds.

The sliding gunter is a good example of the low-tech versatility of traditional sails.

Figure 4-01b

Figure 4-01a

The number of rigging variations with this sail is amazing. The builder can rig the boat with a simple combination of mast, spar, and sail—or a carefully thought-out system

that is perfectly suited to his or her sailing needs. Such a system can be crafted with the builder using nothing more than wood, rope, needle, thread, and marlinspike skills

A gunter yard or spar can be as simple as a square piece of lightweight wood with or without a taper—or, as Willits D. Ansel indicates in *The Whaleboat* (Mystic Seaport Museum, Mystic, Connecticut), even a piece of bamboo. At the other end of the spectrum is the graceful, curved birdwing yard. The use of the curved yard and full-length battens allows this gunter sail to come very close to the RAF Spitfire wing. The Spitfire wing shape provides the most amount of lift with the least amount of induced drag. **Figure 4-02** shows a comparison of the birdwing gunter sail and the elliptical, U-shaped RAF wing. Yet, for all its high-tech appearance, it is nothing more than wood, cloth, and rope.

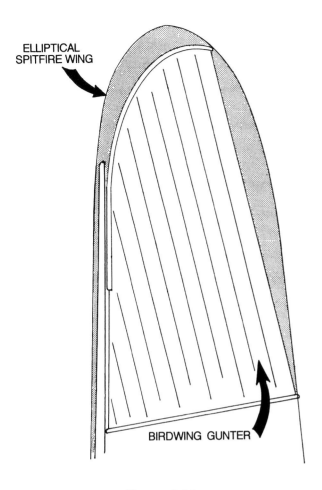

Figure 4-02

Figure 4-03a

Modification doesn't stop with the shape. The yard can use jaws or it can be jawless. The jaws can be wood, plywood, or a simple piece of line. The yards in **Figures 4-03a** and **4-03b** use a simple toggle and a roband—simply a piece of line made fast around a mast or spar with a reef knot (square knot). Both are easy, effective methods of keeping the yard captive at the mast, yet allow the yard to slide freely. If either of these systems is used on boats in the 18- to 20- foot range or larger, it will be better to use parrel beads and service the line. The parrel beads and the stiffness added by the service will help keep the yard from jamming. The Drascombe Longboat, a British 22-foot fiberglass production boat, uses parrel beads with the jaws of its gunter rig (**Figure 4-04**), and even though the jaws are made of metal, the general shape is easy enough to reproduce.

All the rigs, simple and complex, start with the sail laced to the gunter yard. The luff should be tight but not stretched hard. A little experimentation will determine the proper tension. The next step is to lace the sail to the yard. The marlin hitch shown in **Figure 4-05** is probably best if the sail is left bent to the yard. It's fast and holds the

Figure 4-03b

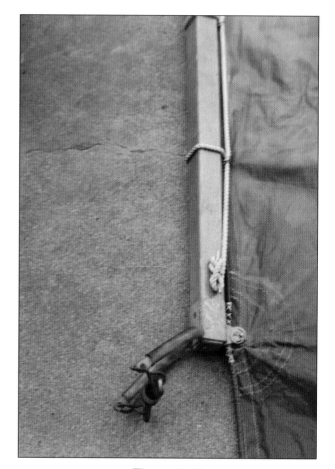

Figure 4-04

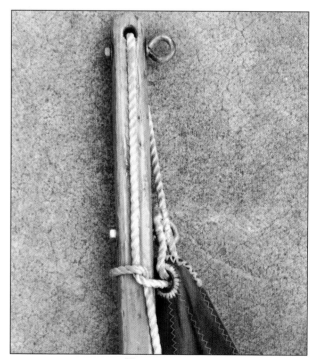

Figure 4-05

sail securely. Actually, there is really no reason to remove the sail each time the boat is used. Round lacing or back-and-forth lacing is faster but doesn't secure the sail as well. Robands can be fast but allow even more sail movement.

Not only are there several possibilities for attaching the sail to the yard, but there are several ways of attaching it to the mast as well. It can be loose-luffed—attached to the mast only at the tack—which accord-

Figure 4-06

ing to Phil Bolger is more correctly a Solent lug sail rather than a gunter variation. Or the luff can be bent on with robands, toggles, or wooden hoops. The Drascombe Longboat uses toggles, which is simple and fast, and the Mirror Dinghy, Jack Holt's famous design, uses lacing. Over 60,000 Mirror Dinghies actively racing means there are a lot of owners lacing the sails to the mast. Other racing designs use tracks to eliminate the gap between the luff and mast. The owner can be as simple or complex as he or she wishes to be.

This variety carries over to the sheeting of the sail as well. There are at least three sheeting possibilities with a loose-footed or boomless sail. A bridle and a single sheet allow the tiller to operate without fouling the mainsheet. A block, brass thimble, or wooden lizard can be used for the sheet to feed through, but a block produces the least drag on the mainsheet. It's also possible to use two mainsheets. The leads can be

as simple as wooden pins or thumb cleats on the rail (**Figure 4-06**) or brass thimbles seized into line. Using two mainsheets has the advantage of allowing the sail to be sheeted past the centerline of the boat—acting like a traveler on a modern rig. While this will improve the boat's pointing ability it adds the complication of more line to tangle. On some boats it may be necessary to use a purchase on the single mainsheet. Most small sails won't need this but if the sail area dictates it, this system will do nicely. The system's main drawback is that the block at the clew can raise a lump on the head of the unwary crew member.

Where the mainsheet lead falls might determine which system is used on the boat. To find the sheeting angle, pick a point in the middle of the luff and imagine a line from there down through the clew to the sheer of the boat. That will be the starting point for the sheeting lead, but some fine-tuning will probably be required.

All the sheeting systems do have one thing in common: The mainsheet is not cleated off. In small boats the sheet should always be in hand to be quickly eased in puffs. And when the puffs get too much to handle, a brailing line provides a fast way to douse the sail without dropping the yard. This useful piece of traditional rigging can be found on several kinds of boomless sails.

On the boomless gunter the brailing line should start at the luff and loop around the

Figure 4-07a

Figure 4-07b

leech to the luff on the other side and then lead aft (**Figure 4-07a**). Brass thimbles sewn to the sail will act as fairleads for the light line.

As the brailing line is hauled in, the loop collapses, pulling the leech to the mast (**Figure 4-07b**). With the sail collapsed against the mast, dropping the yard can wait until a more convenient time. Now the boat can be rowed, work can be done or a sandwich eaten. To get under way again, just reverse the process.

Variations don't stop with the sheeting, as the halyards can be rigged in several ways as well. But regardless of how the halyard is rigged, raising and lowering the sail will be much easier if the halyard is attached at a point that makes the yard bottom-heavy. A bottom-heavy spar will be more likely to behave when it's quickly run

up or lowered.

The simplest system is a single halyard belayed at the mast. The main problem with this occurs when trying to reef the sail. Unless the boat is beached, the spar will start to swing wildly as the halyard is eased to put in the reef. This can be overcome somewhat by adding a toggle below the point the halyard attaches to the spar, as shown in **Figure 4-08**. The toggle holds the yard captive as the reef is put in or the sail dropped. A similar method in **Figure 4-09** is found in John Leather's *Spritsails and Lugsails* (International Marine, Camden, Maine). If the parrel line and hal-

Figure 4-08

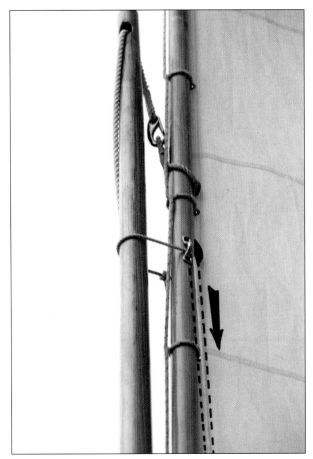

Figure 4-09

yard are led aft and belayed at the center-board trunk, the sail can be raised and lowered from the helm. While this can be an advantage, it does add more line in the boat.

Either method will help control the sail and yard. And control is very important in small boat. The sailing canoes of the 1890s and early 1900s developed quite a few very clever ways of controlling sails as well as yards and quickly shortening sail. Several of these small craft made some impressive and incredible voyages. S. R. Stoddard made a 2,000-mile journey down the Hudson River, up to the Bay of Fundy, through the St. Lawrence Seaway, and back

to Lake Champlain in *Atlantis*, a 20-foot sailing canoe. No less impressive is Frederic Fenger's 500-mile voyage through the Caribbean in his 17-foot *Yakaboo*. These narrow, unballasted, and tender craft demanded almost instant reefing, particularly in the open waters encountered by Stoddard and Fenger. Dixon Kemp in his *Manual of Yacht and Boat Sailing* (New Edition, Ashford Press Publishing, Southampton) details three or four of these types of rigs. A variation on a rig on *Nautilus*, another famous sail canoe of the 1890s, is shown in **Figure 4-10**. Control is provided with two lines, battens, and a

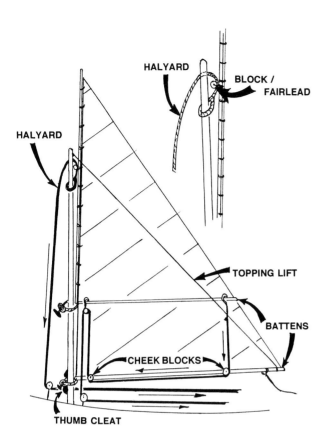

Figure 4-10

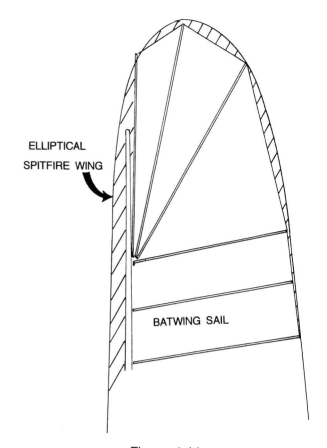

Figure 4-11

topping lift. To reef this sail, the halyard is eased as the reefing line is hauled in and made fast; then a final tug on the halyard tightens the luff.

Sailing canoes of the St. Lawrence River and other areas used another wrinkle called a "batwing" sail. With the addition of no more than two battens, this takes on the highly efficient shape of the RAF wing (**Figure 4-11**). All of this is done with straight battens, a straight gunter yard, and components made by the builder. It looks very similar to sailboard and catamaran sails but predates them by about 100 years.

The batwing and related sails may be too

complicated for the needs of some builders, but just adding a sprit boom to the basic mast, yard, and sail still keeps the system simple. The biggest advantage of the sprit boom is the "self-vanging" effect off the wind. As the mainsheet is eased, the angle of the boom tightens the leech. This helps stop the boat rolling when sailing off the wind. Also, the sprit boom can control the camber of the sail by adjusting the snotter (the line that attaches the sprit boom to the mast). As the wind kicks up, the snotter is hauled in to flatten the sail; the process is reversed to increase the camber in light winds. The photos in **Figures 4-12a** and **4-12b** show a rig that leads the line aft, allowing adjustments to be made from the helm. On larger boats it will probably be necessary to have a purchase on the snotter in order to flatten the sail.

A sprit boom can be added after the fact

Figure 4-12a

Figure 4-12b

to a loose-footed sail, but it's better to decide the way the sail will be rigged before it's ordered or made. A sail for a sprit boom can have a little more camber because the control the sprit offers and the foot will need to be cut flat or with very little round. Obviously, the more complicated the sailing rig, the more information the sail maker will need. The batwing or birdwing gunter will need much more thought from the builder and sail maker than the simple boomless sail.

Also, with a little thought from both the builder and sail maker, a boat that has an existing Bermuda rig can be changed over to a sliding gunter. Because the sails are the same shape, the center of effort will be the same or about the same with both sails. This means the same mast step can be used without changing the balance of the boat. In some cases the existing sail might be re-cut, making the transition even easier. The process is even simpler if the boat is not completed. However, a review of chapter 3 would be in order to avoid changing the balance and performance of the boat.

Figure 4-13 shows the gunter yard of one such conversion with the jaws modeled after the jaws on the Drascombe Longboat. The jaws are ½-inch plywood with a toggle to keep the yard against the mast. **Figure 4-14** is a close-up of the halyard hoist, which is similar to the hoist shown in **Figure 4-10**. The builder took an existing sailing rig that

Figure 4-13
(Photo by Yorgos Papatheododorou)

Figure 4-14
(Photo by Yorgos Papatheododorou)

was awkward and "downright dangerous" and converted it to a rig where he could "rig and unrig the boat single-handed and easily reef the sail" and where "all the spars stow within the boat's length." The owner/builder's assessment of the conversion says it all: "The rig looks great and works beautifully."

So, whether you're retrofitting an existing sail or rigging a new one, the sliding gunter has a great deal to offer. The advantage gained with the short mast and spars

alone make this sail worth considering. But perhaps its greatest appeal is the ability to design and construct a sailing rig that is perfectly suited to your personal needs. Another advantage of the gunter rig—and traditional sails in general—is that they are made by the builder and therefore repairable by the builder. This makes the sliding gunter an efficient and convenient sailing rig.

44

5

THE SPRIT SAIL—
SIMPLE,
EFFICIENT,
AND ELEGANT

Anyone thinking about traditional sails would be hard pressed to find a sail with fewer components than the sprit sail. A rectangular piece of cloth, a mast, a yard (the sprit), a snotter (the line for the sprit), and a mainsheet is all it takes to move a small boat through the water and to the windward (**Figure 5-01**). Yet for so few components the sprit sail can set a very large piece of canvas. That, of course, translates into power to move the boat. Any doubts about the power of this sail will be quickly removed by examining photos of the English sailing barges on the Thames River or the huge sailing barges in Dutch canals. These enormous vessels moved large and heavy cargo through narrow canals and channels, so any sail they carried needed to be weatherly and still keep the decks unencumbered for cargo. In addition, the large mainsail, sometimes 1,200 square feet or so, had to be handled with a small crew. An enormous number of Danish fishing vessels used the advantage of setting a large sail on short spars, as well.

Those wanting scientific rather than anecdotal evidence that the sprit sail is weatherly and efficient will find the research done by Gifford Technology for the United Nations Food and Agriculture Organization and wind tunnel tests done by C. A. Marchaj in the late 1980s very interesting. In the January-February 1990 issue of *WoodenBoat* magazine (#92), Colin

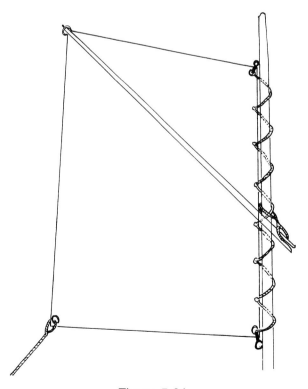

Figure 5-01

Palmer details the results of this testing. According to Palmer, the sprit sail outperformed the ubiquitous Bermudian sail on all points of sail, much to the surprise of many involved in the testing done by Gifford Technology. Marchaj's wind tunnel tests gave the same results.

So why are there so many Bermudian sails and so few sprit sails if the sprit sail is better? The answer lies in racing rules. Everyone sees the Bermudian, or Marconi rig as it's also called, on racing boats and assumes that it is the fastest and most weatherly. However, in the same *WoodenBoat* article, Palmer says that most people "don't realize that the racing rules are actually written to encourage the use of overlapping jibs (genoas) and shorten mainsails (thus the modern Marconi rig) and to penalize the use of other types of rigs."

However, small boats that are unencumbered by racing rules are free to use sails that match more closely the intended use of the boat. The fact that all this simplicity is also very efficient is just icing on the cake.

Also, unlike the Bermudian or Marconi, the sprit sail has no standing rigging—just the round mast and sprit, which can fit inside the boat when struck. And because they are relatively short, both can be easily made from wood. Either solid stock or laminated boards can be used. Fir is good, with spruce being the better and more

expensive choice. In most situations it's doubtful that spruce is worth the extra cost; just good clear stock will do nicely.

Whatever wood is chosen, it's important that the mast be round so it can rotate in the partner. That's about the only thing important about the mast. There are no hard-and-fast rules about the mast or the sprit. R. D. Culler in his book *Skiffs and Schooners* offers this very straightforward formula: "A spritsail mast should not have much taper until near the head; sprits themselves have a taper each way from the middle." He also lists a tapered heel for the mast so the mast can rotate, and he stresses the importance of the mast rotating. It doesn't get much more uncomplicated than that.

A simple sail like the one shown in **Figure 5-01** can be attached to or bent on the mast using several different methods. It can be laced on using a round-and-round, laced with a marlin hitch, or attached with robands or toggles. The tack and throat are made fast in a semi-permanent fashion as the sail is stored wrapped around the mast. This will eliminate the need for a halyard and adds to the sail's simplicity. Whatever method is used to fix the throat and tack to the mast, it should allow for the luff to be pulled tight. A simple line made fast to a cleat on the mast works very well. Putting the line at the tack will allow the luff to be adjusted with the mast stepped.

Figure 5-02a

Setting the sail is also very simple. The sail is unwrapped from the mast and the peak captured, while the sprit is inserted into the becket at the peak. The sprit is pushed upward and the free end is placed in the snotter. If the snotter allows for adjustment, the sprit is sweated up until a crease appears in the sail (**Figures 5-02a, b, c, d**). Now all that remains is to grab the mainsheet and trim the sail to get under way.

All this is very straightforward and very uncomplicated. In some cases the sail is flaked or stored with the sprit attached to the becket. This eliminates having to capture a flogging peak in the wind.

And as with all traditional sails, very complex systems can be built from the simple start. In its most simple form the snotter consists of a single piece of rope with a loop in both ends. One end slips around the mast and rests on a thumb cleat, while the other loop sits in a slot in the end of the sprit. This is quick and effective but doesn't allow for any adjustment of the sprit. A

Figure 5-02b

Figure 5-02c

Figure 5-02d

Figure 5-03

series of thumb cleats allows for the sprit to be sweated up when necessary, but a long strip of hardwood with a series of notches like the one in **Figure 5-03** gives a wider range of adjustment. The sprit in the photo has a short peg with a shoulder rather than a slot or nock. Using a peg with a shoulder is stronger than the slot, but a short peg could jump out of the snotter as the sail flogs in the wind. This clever system was found on a boat at Mystic Seaport Museum.

Another system that allows for sprit adjustment is detailed in chapter 11 of R. D. Culler's *Skiffs and Schooners*. The snotter shown in **Figures 5-04a, b, c** was made from the drawing on page 112 of *Skiffs and Schooners*. It has a long loop created by an eye splice and a brass thimble tightly seized at the base or crotch of the splice. Unlike the

snotter in **Figure 5-03** that stays on the mast, this snotter can be added or removed without unstepping the mast and unlacing the sail. With the snotter in place, the running end of the line is passed through the slot in the sprit and brought back and run through the thimble to be made fast. This allows for the sprit to be sweated up or released quickly. It also gives a purchase, something that will be welcome as it breezes up. If the running end is long enough, it can be led back to the helm and adjustments can be made while under way.

There are many possible variations on this theme. The snotter in **Figure 5-05** has an eye splice in one end and the thimble seized into an eye splice at the other end. A second line has been spliced in above the thimble, fed around the end of the sprit and

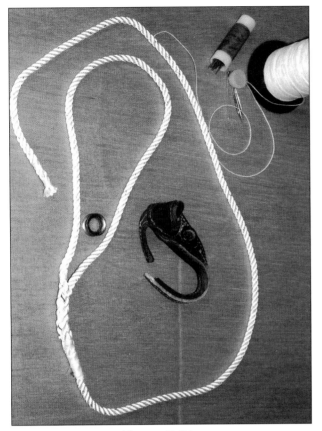

Figure 5-04a

Figure 5-04b

Figure 5-04c

up through the thimble. This might be a better combination if you plan to lead the snotter aft to the helm. Even though there is an additional splice, figuring the length needed to lead aft can be somewhat simpler.

For all the advantages found in its simplicity, the sprit sail does have some disadvantages:

—This is not an easy sail to reef.

—The head of the sail can fall to the leeward when running off, creating the dreaded

Figure 5-05

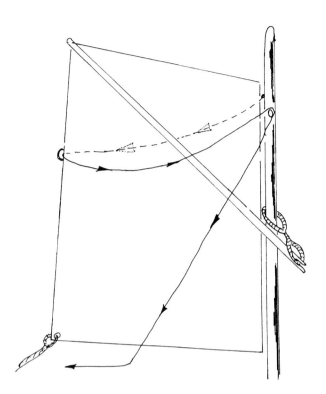

Figure 5-06

rhythmic rolling.

—Sprit and luff tension are critical and require frequent adjustments for the sail to set properly.

—The correct sheeting angle can sometimes be difficult to achieve.

The good news is this sailing rig has been around a long time so there are a great many solutions to the problems.

Probably the simplest solution to reefing the sail in **Figure 5-01** is not to reef. While

this might seem to be a contradiction, it's really not. If the boat is very small or the sail is just an auxiliary to oars, then this is a reasonable option. Sail area should be on the conservative side so the boat is easily handled in winds up to 10 to 12 knots; above that speed the sail is killed and oars are used.

Killing or dousing the sail is accomplished with a brailing line. The line when hauled in collapses the sail and sprit against the mast. Once the sail is captured, the oars are shipped and the boat is gotten under way. For a small open boat this may be the most prudent course of action.

To add a brailing line to the sail: One end of ¼- to 5/16-inch rope is made fast to the mast near the throat, then led through a thimble seized to the leech about two-thirds of the way up between the clew and peak. From the leech the line is fed to a fairlead on the opposite side of the mast and sail, then to the foot of the mast, and then aft within easy reach of the helm (**Figure 5-06**).

To brail up the sail, the mainsheet is eased as the brailing line is hauled in and then made fast. That's it. That's all there is to do. Now the sail will remain killed or doused until the brailing line is released.

There is one more option open to the sail in **Figure 5-01**: scandalizing. Scandalizing the sail is nothing more than removing the sprit and allowing the sail to fold over. Depending on the shape, this will effectively halve the sail (**Figure 5-07**). Capturing the peak at or near the tack will help keep the top half from flogging, and additional capture points will allow the head to be secured to the luff and the leech to the foot. Now the center of effort has been lowered by a couple of feet and the sail considerably de-powered. This configuration will work better off the wind than beating to. It does, however, effectively reduce the sail and help get the boat under control. An adjustable snotter will make the process of scandalizing easier, and practicing under calm and controlled condi-

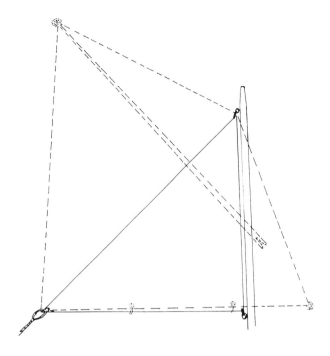

Figure 5-07

tions is a must. Also, scandalizing the sail and other reefing systems will be much easier with the boat beached. There are some who would say this is almost a must.

Any other type of reefing quickly moves from the easy category into the realm of more complicated. The first thing that would have to be changed about the sail in **Figure 5-01** is the addition of a halyard or some method of lowering the throat of the sail. Of course, the throat could no longer be fixed to the mast, and the way the sail is bent on will have to be changed. Robands, toggles, or forth-and-back lacing will be required so the sail can be lowered without jamming. Also, a hole, sheave, or block will have to be added to the top of the mast. The hole, by far the simplest, will need to be relieved on both sides to allow for the halyard to run smoothly and to keep chafe at a minimum on the line.

As the throat is lowered with the halyard, the peak follows, forcing the forward end of the sprit down and sometimes out in front of the mast. If the sprit is too low, the end will strike the deck. This means the location of the sprit without the reef will have take this downward movement into consideration.

Now the new tack at the reef point will need to be made fast to the mast thumb cleat and the mainsheet moved to the reef clew. Then the reef is tucked up with the cringles. Imagine this process being done in a fresh breeze and it's easy to see why the sprit sail has a reputation for being difficult to reef, and why reefing it is considered best done on the beach.

Since each step has so many alternative methods, it can be almost overwhelming. However, it is easier if each step and a few of the options for that step are looked at separately with the knowledge that "mix and match" is the order of the day.

First, it is possible to lower the throat without a halyard. **Figure 5-08** shows a line with both ends made fast at the throat, forming a loop without the reef. The loop is untied and then made fast to the top of the mast when a reef is taken. This method is detailed by Ben Fuller in an article that appeared in the *WoodenBoat* issue of March-April 2002 (#165). It has the

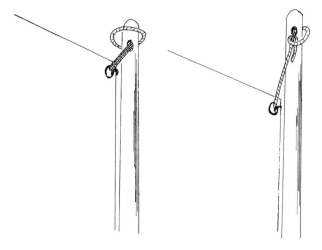

Figure 5-08

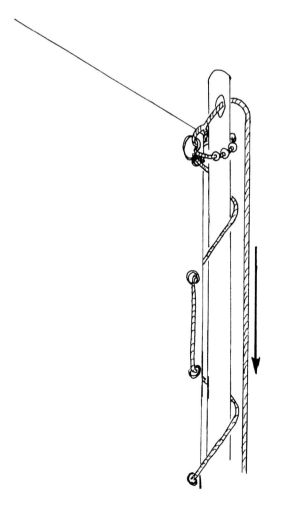

Figure 5-09

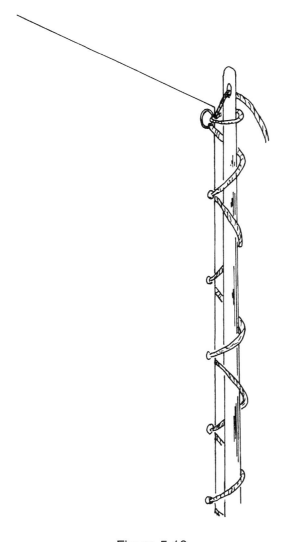

Figure 5-10

Figure 5-11

advantage of keeping a small boat free of an additional line for the halyard but requires the mast to be unstepped.

A simple line through a relieved hole in the top of the mast can be tied off at the mast partner or lead aft (**Figure 5-09**). This creates one more line in the boat but means the mast doesn't have to be lowered to take the reef. Whatever system is used to lead or turn the halyard downward—a relieved hole, block, or sheave—it should run free and allow the sail to come down as well.

Bending the sail on the mast will need to allow for this downward movement. The lacing methods shown in **Figure 5-09** and **Figure 5-10** are less prone to jamming than round-and-round lacing and are probably best if the sail is to stay bent on the mast. Toggles and parrel beads also allow for free movement of the sail. Robands would be the least complicated but the most jam prone.

Accommodating the movement of the sprit seems to have generated some ingenious methods that range from simple to very complex. The snotter in **Figure 5-11** can just be dropped into a lower notch. If a short Culler-type snotter is used, then it can just be repositioned on the mast, either on another thumb cleat or by using a lanyard as in **Figure 5-12**. The lanyard system used by Ben Fuller in *WoodenBoat* #165 eliminates the need for a second thumb cleat—and a second cleat, as he points out, is "one

more thing to foul sail lacings."

If the snotter is led aft, then there are a number of possibilities. Ernie Cassidy, in his article "Sprit Rig Basics" (July-August 1989 *WoodenBoat*, issue #89), just eases the snotter until the sprit can be unshipped, lowers the halyard, ties in the reef, reships the sprit, moves the mainsheet to the reef clew, sweats up the sprit to the proper tension, and gets back under way. **Figure 5-13** shows that the sprit moves downward with the extra length of the snotter. Doing all of the above in a small boat in the middle of a lake full of whitecaps would be unpleasant at best. It's easy to see why he strongly suggests that reefing on the beach be "an ironclad rule."

Figure 5-12

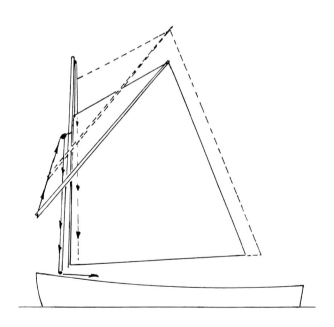

Figure 5-13

The drawing in **Figures 5-14a** and **b** show two more methods of dealing with sprit movement. **Figure 5-14a** is a composite from an Iain Oughtred article in *WoodenBoat* magazine, photos and drawings of Thames River barges and drawings of Danish fishing boats. This system just lowers the sprit and doesn't allow for the sprit to move outward from the mast. It has the advantage of keeping the heel of the sprit captured next to the mast, but the toggles or lacing will need to be placed to avoid fouling the parrel beads or collar as the sail is lowered.

Figure 5-14b, taken from John Leather's *Spritsails and Lugsails*, has the sprit attached with a snotter that doesn't move. The sail is lowered with a throat halyard and a peak halyard. As the sail is lowered, a topping lift attached to the sprit is eased and the mainsheet moved to the reef clew.

Both these systems lend themselves to boats in the 18-to-26-foot range or larger where the extra lines and rigging aren't as much of an issue. **Figure 5-14b**, according to Leather, was found on fishing vessels of the Baltic where beaching to reef just wasn't possible.

How did these fishing boats manage in places like the Baltic and North Sea? It is possible, of course, to reef a sprit sail at sea, and fishing boats did just that, but there are some other options open to larger boats. Many boats carried a main with a jib

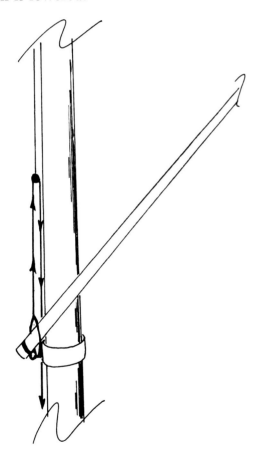

Figure 5-14a

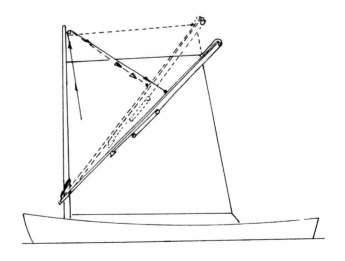

Figure 5-14b

as well as a mizzen; some even carried three masts. To shorten sail, the jib or mizzen is struck; then the remaining smaller sail, then reef the main, then strike the main and replace it with the mizzen or any combination of the above.

Boats working with just a main, jib, and mizzen could start with the mainsail on the smallish side and set a topsail as in **Figure 5-15**. As the wind increases, the topsail is struck, and then various combinations of sail reductions are made. Even a boat under 16 feet using a split rig could apply the same thinking: First strike the topsail, then scandalize the main, then strike the mizzen, then strike the scandalized main and replace it with the mizzen. If the builder chooses not to have a mizzen, the topsail can be struck, then the jib; then scandalize the main. All this can be done

without having to take a reef.

There are two other options that are worth studying: a divided rig designed in 1935 and a lowerable, reefable sprit sail shown in Dixon Kemp's *Manual of Yacht and Boat Sailing* from the turn of the 20th century. Both sails are complicated but show how the sprit rig can be varied to suit individual purposes.

The divided rig, developed in Great Britain by H. Banbury and shown on page 61 of John Leather's *Spritsails and Lugsails*, divides the main sail in two separate sails (**Figure 5-16**). Here the sprit is more of a vertical boom and uses a gooseneck rather than a snotter to capture it. Also, the line and tackle that runs from the end of the sprit to the stern acts as a vang for the sprit. And while the sail is perhaps too complex for a small boat, the variation shown in

Figure 5-15

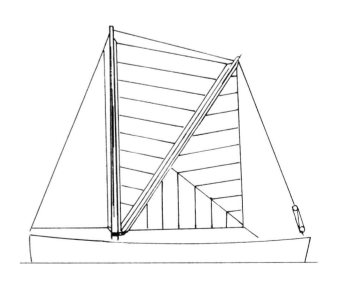

Figure 5-16

Figure 5-17 might be very useful. Instead of two sails, the sprit sits in a pocket with the heel attached to the mast with a gooseneck. The lift is made fast to the sprit and led down the mast and aft to the helm. This becomes a brailing line that halves the sail when hauled in and captures it like lazy jacks. Once brailed up, the mainsheet is moved farther aft and the boat continues on. A second brailing line can be set to brail up the top third of the lower portion for a second reef. The use of a second brailing line can be seen on photos of sailing barges on the Thames. In order for this system to work, the mast must sit far enough forward to allow for the change in the sheeting angle each time the sail is brailed. In most cases the sheeting point will fall too far aft of the stern, but if there is a mizzen sail the sheeting point can be moved to the mizzenmast.

The Dixon Kemp sail shown in **Figure 5-18a** was used on the sailing canoe *Nautilus* in the late 1880s. He lists this sail as being about 70 to 80 square feet—which is sizable considering *Nautilus* was only 14 feet long and had a beam of less than 36 inches. The two sets of reef points effectively halve the sail, but that still leaves about 40 square feet of sail. **Figure 5-18b** shows first haul on the halyard.

Because the sprit, *spreet* as Kemp spelled it, is in a pocket (like the variation in **Figure 5-17**), it moves straight down as the sail is reefed. However, this sail, unlike any discussed so far, uses a boom. If the sail were boomless the sheeting angle, determined by bisecting the angle made by the foot and leech, would fall too far aft, but the use of

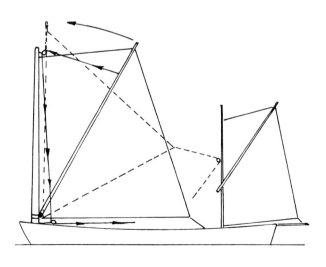

Figure 5-17

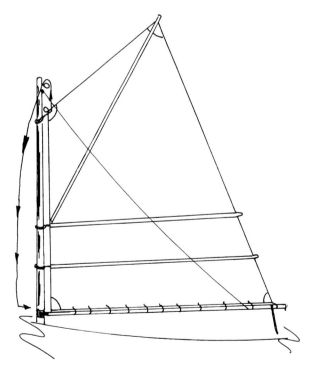

Figure 5-18a

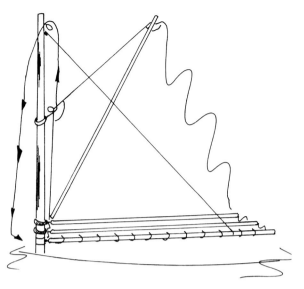

Figure 5-18b

Figure 5-19

a boom allows the mainsheet to be placed in a more convenient place. The boat in **Figure 5-19** had the same problem. Cutting the sail with the clew higher for better visibility caused the sheeting angle to fall well aft of the stern.

In a small boat a boom solves one problem but creates others. Not only does the boom have to be watched carefully as the boat tacks, but it is more difficult to brail as well. A sail with a boom can be brailed, but the boom jaws will have to allow for the upward movement.

Just as the Kemp sail uses a boom to solve a problem, Banbury's experimental sail uses vangs to solve another. In Banbury's sail the vangs were led to the deck right at the stern. This vang, when hauled in, limited the forward movement of the peak and helped stop the rhythmic rolling this sail can develop. Photos of the Thames River barges show that

vangs led to the mizzen and to the deck. Looking at a large number of photos of these barges, virtually all of them had some sort of vang system. This would seem to indicate the importance of controlling the sprit at the peak in order to maintain proper sail shape.

In general, controlling the sprit is critical to proper sail shape, as well as luff tension and sheeting angle. All of these are in a constant state of flux as the boat moves through the water. If squeezing every last drop of performance is important, then it will be necessary for the owner to have a complex system to make those adjustments. If simplicity is the goal, then the sail in **Figure 5-01** will do very well; in fact, there may be none better.

6

LUG SAILS

Traditional working sails had to meet several criteria in order to gain widespread acceptance. Simplicity was a major consideration, because it was not unusual for a person wanting to earn a living from the sea to build his own boat. This meant making everything on the boat, including the running and standing rigging and occasionally even the sails.

Dependability was another important factor that needed to be met by traditional sails. Traditional sails needed to work as well during a gale as they did in a gentle breeze. If they broke, they needed to be repaired by the owner while at sea if the need arose. They had to get the owner to and from the market in a timely manner, even if it meant sailing to the windward. In general, sails had to meet the needs of those whose lives and livelihoods depended on the sea.

Lug sails met those needs for a very long

time. A look at early paintings and photographs of fishing boats, large and small, shows lug sails driving them. A very large number of British fishing boats were still using dipping lug sails as late as the 1880s. Many of these boats were 70 to 80 feet long, and required a great deal of power to pull long nets.

Providing power is what a dipping lug sail does best. It would be difficult to find a rig that can set as much sail on such a short mast and with as little standing rigging. But all that canvas comes at a fairly significant trade-off—it's rather cumbersome to tack. Bringing the boat about and through the eye of the wind requires the crew to free the tack of the sail, bring it around the mast, and reattach the tack so the sail and the yard lie to the lee of the mast. This is an operation not easily accomplished single-handed or by a shorthanded crew, and, in general, the dipping lug rig doesn't lend itself to small boats.

However, other types—the standing lug and the balanced lug—are simple and efficient rigs that do work very well on small boats. Either rig can be set on a short mast and yard, with a minimum of running rigging and no standing rigging. Each has it own advantages with very few disadvantages.

The standing lug (**Figure 6-01**) has the tack just aft of the mast and can be set with or without a boom. In the most simple form, all that is required is sail, mast, yard,

Figure 6-01

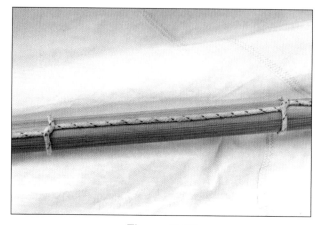

Figure 6-02

Figure 6-03

halyard, and mainsheet—all of which will move the boat to the windward in a very reliable fashion, and when struck will fit neatly inside the boat.

In all rigs, both simple and complex, the sail is made fast to the yard. The throat is fixed at one end of the yard, stretched taut, and the peak is lashed to the yard. The head of the sail is then bent onto the yard by several methods. Generally, marlin hitch lacing (**Figure 6-02**) will fit most needs, but robands or round-and-round lacing can also be used.

Just as there are several methods to bend on the sails, there are several options for attaching the halyard to the yard. The most straightforward uses a rolling hitch to fasten the halyard to the yard (**Figure 6-03**).

Another system is a rope and thimble seized to the yard, with the halyard having a hook or just made fast through the thimble. A thumb cleat on the yard will secure the rope and thimble and keep it from sliding on the yard. Any number of alternatives can be used, but the halyard should be easily separated from the yard.

Where the halyard is attached is more

Figure 6-04

important than *how* it is attached because the placement will determine how well the sail sets. According to John Leather in *Spritsails and Lugsails*, the placement will vary anywhere from one-fourth to three-eighths from the forward end on the yard, but one-third seems to be the best starting point. It's good to remember that if the halyard is attached too far back, proper luff tension will be difficult to archive. Because each sail is different, however, it will take some experimenting to find the proper point on the yard. Once found, a mark will ensure the halyard is bent on at the same point every time.

Finding the proper angle for the sheet lead will also take some experimentation. A good method for determining a starting point is to bisect the angle made by the foot and the leech. Then extend a line down to the sheer of the boat (**Figure 6-04**). According to *Spritsails and Lugsails*, this should be roughly 2½ feet forward of the transom on a 16-foot boat. That figure is by no means exact, and in order for the sail to work best there must be fairly even tension on the foot and the leech. Also, the sheeting angle may change slightly with wind speed and as the boat moves from a beat to a reach, so it is best to experiment with several points before settling on the final one.

Using several sheeting points rather than a single point will be easier if two mainsheets are used instead of using one mainsheet. With two sheets, points along the rail can be picked, and thimbles, bull's-eyes, or cleats can be made fast to those spots. Moving the slack sheet up and down the rail will allow the sheeting angle to be changed as conditions dictate. This system will have the added benefit of being able to sheet the clew past the centerline of the boat. **Figure 6-05** shows a series of rail cleats that provide for two sheets as well as a single sheet.

A single mainsheet does have several advantages, but unless the sheeting points fall aft of the tiller, a bridle or horse may have to be used. While it is possible to switch a single mainsheet from side to side,

Figure 6-05

Figure 6-06

it entails quite a bit of juggling, and the bridle will help keep the sheet from fouling the tiller every time the boat is tacked. A bridle with a thimble or bull's-eye will do the job nicely and can be made by the builder. A block will, of course, let the mainsheet run more easily and with less friction. In any case, the mainsheet should not be made fast or cleated off, so it can be released in a gust. This becomes increasingly more important as the size of the boat decreases. The amount of clutter seems to increase geometrically as the boat length shortens, so less line provided by the single mainsheet means less clutter. And, of course, there is 50 percent less line to buy.

Like all traditional sails, this simple rig lends itself to experimentation and adaptation to individual needs using just wood,

rope, needle, sewing palm, and marlinspike skills. Each addition and adaptation made by the owner increases the ease of handling, but also increases the complexity and cost.

The first addition will become obvious the first time the yard lies on the lee side of the mast. Even with a great deal of tension on the luff, the yard will not lie against the mast. It will have a tendency to flail about, creating problems as the halyard is released and the yard lowered. This problem is easily solved with a parrel line that captures the yard against the mast. Over the years a

Figure 6-07

Figure 6-08

number of solutions have evolved, but one of the simplest uses a toggle attached to the yard (**Figure 6-06**). The toggle is made fast around the mast at the time the halyard is attached to the yard.

John Leather details several other methods in *Spritsails and Lugsails*. The simplest of these is a thimble seized to the yard at the point where the halyard would be attached. The line is fed through the thimble, around the mast, and made fast at the yard's heel. This way the halyard acts as the parrel line (**Figure 6-07**). A variation on this uses a line that is separate from the halyard. It is belayed to the yard above the halyard, led around the mast and down to a cleat to a thimble, and then down to a cleat at the base of the mast. In **Figure 6-08** a separate line is attached with a rolling hitch led around the mast and then made fast with another rolling hitch. The most complex method has the halyard attached

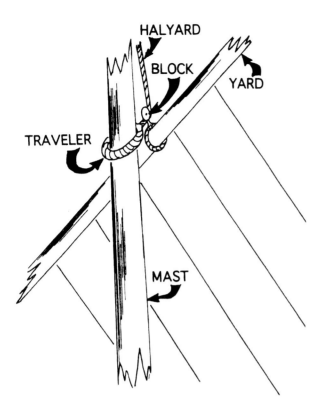

Figure 6-09

Figure 6-10

to a traveler around the mast, then fed through a block attached to the yard and then up to the sheave at the top of the mast (**Figure 6-09**). This system, also detailed in Dixon Kemp's *Manual of Yacht and Boat Sailing*, was used on sailing canoes of the 1890s. All of these methods will do the job well and can be expanded or simplified according to the whim of the owner.

The next addition should be a downhaul with a purchase (**Figure 6-10**). This piece of gear will make a marked improvement in the windward performance of the boat. Set the sail with the luff tight, and then apply tension to luff with the downhaul. If there is enough of a purchase, it is possible to be too zealous with the downhaul and drive the

mast through the bottom of the boat. This can have a damping effect on the day's sailing, so care should be exercised.

The extra stress on the luff caused by the downhaul also creates the need to reinforce the luff with an extra tabling or luff rope. The reinforcing will take the load off the sailcloth and increase the life of the sail.

The downhaul itself can be easily made by the builder with rope and thimbles or just rope. Blocks will certainly do the job, but for a small boat even simple rope loops will provide the necessary purchase. Eye splices and leather will give a seaman-like look to the boat, and the leather will help prevent chafe. The downhaul in **Figure 6-10** uses rope and thimbles to give a 1:1 purchase. The brass thimbles not only stop any chafing but also help the rope run smoothly. A bull's-eye, made from a hard-wood sanded and waxed smooth, will also allow the line an easy run. Using more than a 2:1 purchase definitely falls into the overkill category for small boats, thereby increasing the chances of forcing the mast through the bottom.

While the downhaul will be critical to windward performance, a dipping line is another piece of rigging that will improve performance. The gains achieved with the dipping line will not be as great as with the downhaul, but it does serve a useful function. As the boat is tacked back and forth through the eye of the wind, the yard will be on either the windward side or leeward side of the mast. When the yard is on the windward side, the mast will press against the luff and disrupt the airflow. A dipping line allows the yard to be switched or dipped so it is always on the lee side of the mast. Also, keeping the yard on the lee side keeps the wind from jamming the yard against the side of the mast, making it difficult to drop the sail should the need arise.

All the maneuvering is accomplished

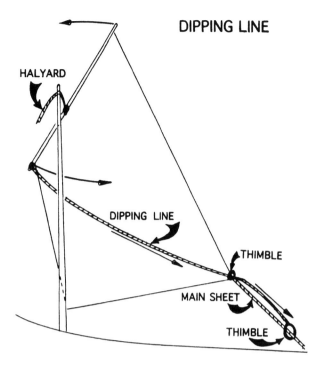

Figure 6-11

with a single line attached to the heel of the yard and led across the belly of the sail to the clew so it can be reached easily by the helmsman (**Figure 6-11**). The whole process is undertaken as the bow comes through the eye of the wind and the sail starts to luff. Then the line is pulled so the heel of the yard drops behind the mast and is pushed to the lee side by the wind. Attaching the line to the mainsheet with an eye splice or thimble lets the line slice, but keeps it handy and clear of the inside of the boat.

While the dipping line will prove helpful with the operation of the boat, a brailing line will be indispensable. The brailing line provides a fast and easy way to kill the sail simply by collapsing it against the yard and mast. The boat can be rowed, a nap taken,

Figure 6-12a

Figure 6-12b

or the boat beached without having to lower the sail into the boat. Getting under way again means just releasing the brailing line and hauling in on the mainsheet. The price tag for all this convenience is only two thimbles and several feet of light line. One end of the line is made fast at the heel of the yard, fed through a thimble sewn to the leech of the sail (a grommet in the tabling will also work), then run down the opposite side of the sail to a thimble seized to the heel of the yard (**Figure 6-12a**). From here, the line is run to a fairlead at the base of the mast, and then aft to with-

in easy reach of the helm (**Figure 6-12b**). If the sail is kept on the same side of the mast as the yard, then the sail can be brailed up and the yard dropped. This will be important if the sheet has been let go in a gust and the sail needs to come down in a hurry. The unbrailed sail will have a tendency to wind up in the water as the yard is dropped, but a brail sail will be more likely to stay in the boat.

Brailing a boomed sail is a completely different matter, and, while it can be done, the process is much more difficult. The first method involves making the line fast on the end of yard at the throat and running it to the aft end of the boom near the clew. From here, the line is fed through a fairlead on the underside of the boom and up the opposite side of the sail to a fairlead at the top of the mast. The line is passed through this fairlead and down to a fairlead at the base of the mast, where it runs aft to the helm. The brailing line acts like lazy jacks, and helps contain the sail as it is collapsed between the boom and the mast.

Of course the mainsheet must run free during this process or the boom's upward travel will come to an abrupt halt. This system can be used on either a loose-footed sail or a sail bent on the boom. Another system depends on the sail being loose-footed. Here the clew outhaul is released as the brailing line is hauled in. Both methods are complex, and that complexity may outweigh any benefits gained from being able to brail the sail.

Booms themselves can be a great complication in a small boat. An unexpected jibe can raise a significant lump on an unwary sailor's head, and tacking generally means ducking as the boom sweeps across the boat. Booms do, however, improve performance and provide another means of adjusting the sail. The boom on a standing lug sail requires a jaw, but there are several simple possibilities. The most simple is a toggle or roband to hold the boom against the mast. Jaws aren't terribly difficult to

Figure 6-13

make and will be more likely to improve the performance of the boat. The jaws in **Figure 6-13** are fir with 1/8-inch veneer laminated to each side for extra strength. Regardless of the type of jaw used, a parrel line will help keep it captive against the mast. The system in **Figure 6-13** has the tack and downhaul secured to the boom, along with a parrel line (not visible in the photo) to keep it all captive.

This system can use a loose-footed sail or a sail laced to the boom. The Cadet Dinghy, a 12-foot racer, uses a sail laced to the boom, but a loose-footed sail would allow for a substantial increase in the foot roach not allowed by the Cadet's one-design rules. Both have advantages as well as disadvantages, and the boat owner not bound by one-design rules should experiment to see which best meets his or her needs.

Whether the sail is loose-footed or not, with or without a boom, there will come a time when the wind pipes up and the need to shorten sail becomes a pressing issue. The shore is the best place to reduce sail, which means taking the advice that "the best time to reef is when you first think you might need to." If the situation becomes completely unmanageable, the sail can be brailed up, or the yard dropped and the boat rowed to shore where the reef can be put in safely. For a standing lug, this involves lowering the yard so the reef tack can be secured and moving the mainsheet to the reef clew. The foot is folded up and made fast with reef nettles, and then the halyard is reset. With the halyard snubbed up, the downhaul is tightened and the boat is made ready to sail (**Figure 6-14**). On shore and in a fresh breeze, this process can be trying, but adrift in the middle a large body of water covered in whitecaps, it can create a major flow of adrenaline. Also, this is not the place or time to try reefing for the first time.

In some cases the balanced lug sail

Figure 6-14

(**Figure 6-15**), with its tack and a portion of the boom in front of the mast, is much easier to reef than the standing lug sail. A system of lines, battens, and blocks (**Figure 6-16**) can reduce sail very quickly by hauling in on one line and releasing another. Dixon Kemp's *Manual of Yacht and Boat Sailing* details several methods used by the racing canoes of the 1880s and 90s. These systems can also be used on the standing lug sail with great success—if that sail carries a boom. The complexity of lines and blocks won't lend itself to every boat, but in many cases the convenience of virtually instant reefing will outweigh that complexity.

Another virtue of the balanced lug sail lies in its downwind ability. Having some of the sail in front of the mast tends to take some of the power out of a jibe. According to John Leather's *Spritsails and Lugsails*, the

BALANCED LUG SAIL

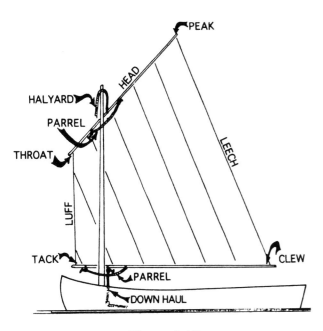

Figure 6-15

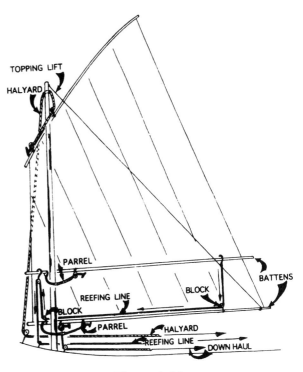

Figure 6-16

area in front of the mast shouldn't exceed about one-seventh of the foot. More can cause problems as the boat tries to luff up in a heavy wind. Also, the area in front of the downhaul helps keep the leech tight off the wind. This self-vanging ability somewhat dampens rhythmic rolling and makes downwind runs more enjoyable.

Both balanced lugs and standing lugs can be crosscut or vertically cut. The vertical cut (panels parallel to the leech) is more traditional in appearance, but offers no advantage to panels at 90 degrees to the leech or to a crosscut sail. Some sail makers feel that the crosscut sail is easier to make than a vertically cut sail, because it allows for easier broadseaming. However, in most cases, the whim of the boat owner will

determine the cut of the sail.

The advantages of the lug sail can be demonstrated by using the Cadet racing dinghy as an example. This little boat sets a total of 176 square feet of sail with a standing lug rig. A 93-square-foot main, 33-square-foot jib, and 50-square-foot spinnaker are all flown on mast and spars under 11 feet long. A Bermuda rig would require an 18-foot mast, 10-foot boom, and considerable standing rigging to fly the same area. While some would argue that a Bermuda rig points higher and is faster on a beat, the offwind ability and other advantages of the lug sails demonstrate they can get the job done—and do so traditionally.

7

THE CHINESE
LUG SAIL

For the owner/builder wanting a weatherly, efficient, and easily handled sailing rig, the Chinese lug sail is a good choice. Really a balanced lug sail with vangs and battens, the Chinese lug sail has been moving boats, both large and small, through the water for a very long time. It may be more accurate to say the balanced lug sail is really a Chinese lug sail without the vangs and battens. Just like spaghetti is really a Chinese noodle imported by Marco Polo.

The sail was used with great success by H. G. "Blondie" Hasler on his Folkboat *Jester* in a number of OSTAR races. Hasler, in the first race, beat another Folkboat using a modified Cutter rig by number of days. Yet despite the publicity given the sail by Hasler, and its history of several thousand years, this sail has been all but ignored in America and Europe.

This is even harder to understand when you examine the reasons Hasler settled on the Chinese lug sail for his 25-foot-long Folkboat. According to Sheila McCurdy in a 1993 *WoodenBoat* article, Hasler choose the sail because it could be handled at all times without going on deck. He found it was more self-tending and easier to reef than other sails he tried, and it could be reefed one panel at a time. Also, there was no need for a large battery of sails because one sail worked for all conditions.

All these reasons would appeal to a small-boat builder not restricted by racing or one-design rules. It is interesting to note

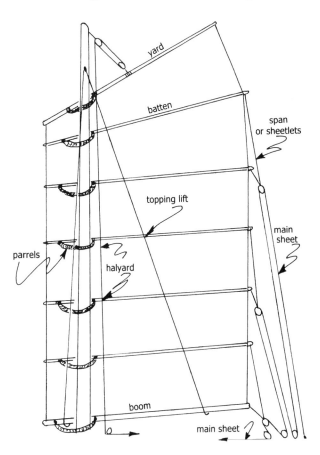

Figure 7-01

that after a large number of transatlantic crossings *Jester*'s rig has remained virtually unchanged.

So what is it that makes this sail work so well? The sail in **Figure 7-01** may look more like a spiderweb than a sail and it is possible the sheets, halyard, topping lifts, and batten downhauls are what sailors find intimidating. However, the sheet and sheet spans or sheetlets all lead to a single sheet to control the boom; there is just a single halyard; the topping lift, which also functions as a lazy jack, is generally belayed and left alone; and there are just one or two batten downhauls. This is really no more lines than a sloop or cutter rig, and the Chinese lug sail's mast is unstayed so that eliminates the standing rigging of the sloop or cutter. Like any unstayed mast, however, it will have to be firmly attached to the partner or step.

The lack of standing rigging not only creates less hull stress—important on a small, lightly built boat—but there is less weight aloft. The Chinese lug sail can be heavy because of the number of battens and running rigging, so the lack of standing rigging can offset that weight. If care is taken to make the mast, battens, and running rigging lightweight but strong, then the low center of effort of the sail combined with absence of standing rigging means less heeling than a conventional sail.

Also, without standing rigging, the sail is free to weathervane and swing out perpendicular to the centerline on a dead run downwind. Those downwind runs are safer because an accidental jibe poises no threat to nonexistent standing rigging. And because the Chinese lug sail has a portion of the sail in front of the mast, those jibes are somewhat de-powered as well.

The downwind runs are also helped because the sail's self-vanging ability limits the rhythmic rolling. The area in front of the mast helps make it, like the balanced lug it is, self-vanging. But it is the sheets and sheet spans that really do the main job of controlling sail shape. The multiple sheets and sheet spans attached to the end of the battens act like the single or double vangs of the sprit sail, except they do a better job because there are more of them. This will translate into better performance.

The battens do more than just give the sheets and sheet spans (sheetlets) something to attach to; they define the shape of the sail, make reefing a piece of cake, and distribute the stress load on the sailcloth.

It is the battens rather than broadseaming that define the sail shape for a Chinese lug sail. This means the sail is cut flat with the panels sewn together straight edge to straight edge. An examination of photos of working Chinese junks shows the panels vertical and parallel to the mast (**Figure 7-02**). Derek Van Loan in his book *The Chinese Sailing Rig* (Paradise Cay

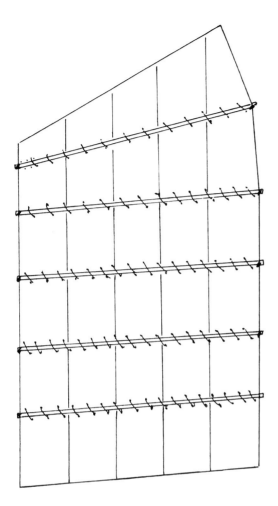

Figure 7-02

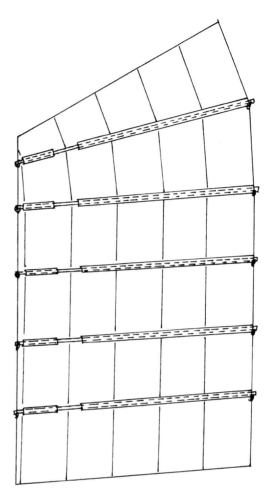

Figure 7-03

Publications, Middletown, California) also prefers this cloth layout. This is the easiest for the builder with no sail-making experience. The panels are sewn together, and then the battens are attached with lacing. Van Loan discourages the use of batten pockets, as he feels these are difficult to replace or repair at sea. H. G. Hasler, in *Practical Junk Rig* (Tiller Publishing, St. Michaels, Maryland) on the other hand shows batten pockets and the cloth parallel with the leech (**Figure 7-03**). Builders planning on sewing their own sail might be

better served with simpler method of **Figure 7-02**.

Whether the batten is in a pocket or just laced to the sail, it will have to be stiff enough to resist bending into an S curve as the wind speed increases (**Figure 7-04**). Van Loan suggests that a fir or spruce batten 5 to 10 feet in length have a depth of 1 5/8 inches and a thickness of ½ to 1 inch. *Practical Junk Rig* uses a complex system for determining batten size and suggests an asymmetrical batten—which may be more work than the small-boat builder wants.

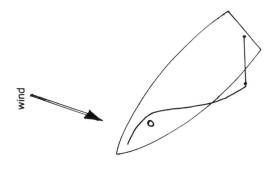

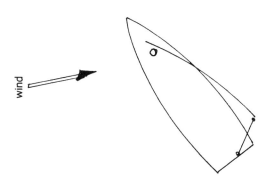

Figure 7-04

Adding lightweight fiberglass cloth to both sides of a wooden batten as suggested by Hasler would be easy enough and add stiffness to the batten while allowing a smaller and lighter size. Certainly other materials can be used for battens like bamboo or cane, but both Van Loan and Hasler feel that PVC pipe is not an acceptable batten material because it's heavy and lacks the required stiffness.

And weight is an issue, as the battens are responsible for most of the weight of the Chinese lug sail. It is this weight that makes reefing so easy. Let the halyard go and this sail drops like the proverbial lead balloon. Ease the halyard down and the sail

drops into the topping lifts one panel at a time. Then just belay the batten downhaul, sweat up the halyard, and the reef is tucked in. There is no luffing up, no having to struggle with the downhaul of a jiffy reefing system, and no cringles to tie off while sliding around on a wet and pitching deck. Just let go of the halyard and this sail rushes down.

To shake out the reef, all that is necessary is to reverse the process. First, let go the batten downhaul, sweat up the halyard as the sail comes up one panel at a time, belay the downhaul, give the halyard one more tug if required, and it's done. Hauling in on the halyard will make the builder very happy that effort was made to make those battens as light and strong as possible. Also, because the battens distribute the stress loads over the sail, a lighter-weight sailcloth can be used. This means that ever-present blue tarp could be used with satisfactory results for the builder wanting to reduce costs and willing to ignore aesthetics.

If care has been taken to make everything lightweight and strong, then the advantages of no standing rigging and lighter sailcloth combined with the lower center of effort of the sail mean the boat will heel less for a given wind speed.

However, to take advantage of all the benefits of this sail does require more planning than with some other traditional sails. This is because there are just more parts and variations to this sail than many other traditional sails.

While an enormous variation in the shape of the sail can be found in Chinese and Asian waters, both Hasler and Van Loan feel the shape in **Figure 7-01** is the optimum. Hasler shows a bit more rise to the yard and *Jester*'s sail has a bit more roach to the luff, but they both feel that this basic shape is best.

Practical Junk Rig uses a series of tables and formulas to determine the angles of tack and throat and the aspect ratio of the sail, while *The Chinese Sailing Rig* uses a simple approach. Van Loan says the angle at the tack should be 85 to 90 degrees, the angle of the throat should be 125 degrees and the foot should be equal to .66 to 1.2 times the luff. The .66 number will give a higher-aspect sail (the foot of the sail shorter than the luff), and the 1.2 number will give a sail that is low aspect (the foot longer than the luff). Practical experience suggests that a sail with its final shape close to **Figure 7-01** will perform well, and a sail that deviates too far in either direction will give less satisfactory results. So care should be taken to achieve a final shape close to what Hasler and Van Loan consider the optimum.

And it is the shape of the sail that determines how the battens will lay in the topping lift. Hasler feels this is important enough to devote an entire chapter in

Practical Junk Rig to sail shape and the way battens stack into the topping lift. He examines in great detail how different sail shapes affect the way the battens stack. The sail in **Figure 7-01** will stack each batten with its end aft of the batten below, as it is furled. This is critical for the sail to be self-tending, and Hasler points out that this keeps the sheets and sheet spans from fouling on the batten below as the sail is raised.

He also points out that the angle of the battens to the luff, which is parallel to the mast, will affect how they stack as well. If the battens are attached to the sail rather than in pockets, it will be easier to make an adjustment should it be required.

Not using pockets would have another benefit. The number of battens could be changed without a great deal of work after the sail has been tested on the boat. Hasler seems to prefer six interior battens while Van Loan favors five, up to 200 square feet of sail. From 200 to 700 square feet he recommends six. Generally, in the case of a small sail, less will be more. The advantages of less load on the cloth and more control of the sail provided by the extra panel will not outweigh the disadvantage of the additional sheet and sheet spans.

Once the number of battens has been established, the next step is to determine where the mast will fall on the sail and add the parrels. Care should be taken to not have too much area in front of the mast, as this will cause problems as the boat tries to luff up in heavy winds. Figures for how much area in front of the mast seem to vary. John Leather suggests the mast placement should be about one-seventh of the length of the foot for a balanced lug sail, while *Practical Junk Rig* feels that about 10 percent of the overall sail area forward of the mast is best, but gives a range of 5 to 30 percent as acceptable. Van Loan seems to prefer a larger amount and recommends 25 percent in front of the mast. *Jester's* balance has remained unchanged at 22 percent, but later sails designed by Hasler trend toward a smaller amount of balance. Practical experience with balanced lug sails by this author suggests that Leather's amount is on the very low side and that a balance area of 10 to 15 percent will give the best performance. One of the advantages of the Chinese lug sail is the adjustability of the balance area. Simple adjustments of the parrels allow the amount to be slowly tweaked as experience dictates for the individual hull.

Where the halyard attaches to the yard will also take some experimenting. In a balanced lug sail a good starting point is about a third of the length of the yard from the forward end and this will certainly work for the Chinese lug sail. However, placing the halyard just aft of where the mast will cross the yard may be a better starting point. This can be determined from the

scaled drawing made to design the sail and calculate the balance. It should be remembered that placing the halyard too far aft will result in poor luff tension. But Van Loan seems to consistently place the halyard farther aft on the yard than Hasler. Wherever the halyard is attached, it should not bind as the sail roates from starboard jibe to port jibe. A day with calm winds and the boat on a trailer will be best for this kind of experimenting.

As with the balanced lug sail, there can be a wide variation of parrel types on a Chinese lug sail. If no batten pocket is used then just attaching the parrel to the batten at one end and a rolling hitch at the other will serve very well until the final positions are determined. A rolling hitch at both ends will allow the maximum flexibility. The placement of the parrel aft of the mast will be more important than the placement on the luff side. The parrel not only keeps the sail against the mast but also stops it from slumping forward. The forward movement causes a roach in the luff and a hollow in the leech, and this in turn spoils the shape of the sail.

Once the proper balance and placement have been established, then the ends of the parrel can be permanently attached to the batten. Even on a small sail the addition of parrel beads or balls will ease the hoisting and dropping of the sail. On a small sail that will not stay attached to the mast, a toggle

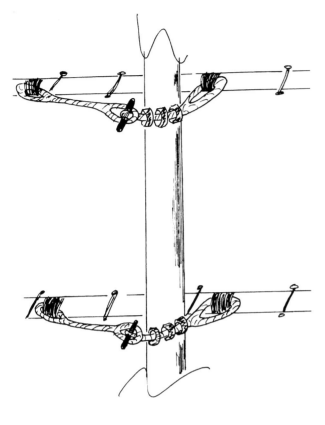

Figure 7-05

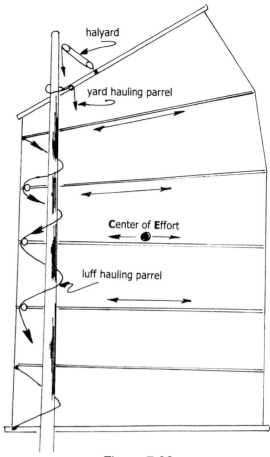

Figure 7-06

seized to the batten, as in **Figure 7-05**, will allow the sail to be easily attached and removed from the mast.

The parrel system shown in **Figure 7-05** will serve very well on small to medium sized sails, but on large sails or sails that will stay permanently attached to the mast it would be best to seize both ends of the parrel to the batten. *The Chinese Sailing Rig* shows a parrel line seized at both ends on the boom, battens and yard, a simple and straightforward system as in **Figure 7-01**.

Practical Junk Rig, on the other hand, has a number of methods including the luff-hauling line in shown **Figure 7-06**. As the line is hauled in, the luff is pulled aft,

forcing some shape into the battens and moving the center of effort of the sail aft as well. In most cases, however, this will prove too complicated for all but those wishing to squeeze every ounce of performance from the sail.

Actually, an adjustment in the amount of balance will also affect the movement of the center of effort—less balance forward of the mast moves the COE aft, while more balance forward of the mast moves the COE forward (**Figure 7-06**). This will be very important in how the helm balances and gives a method of correcting excessive weather or lee helm.

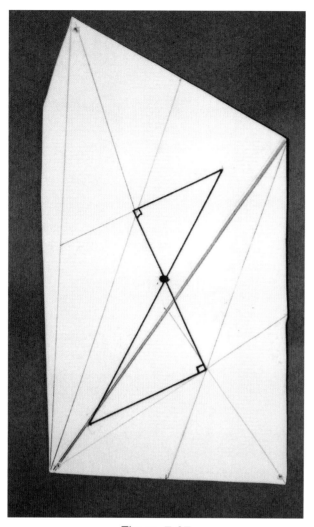

Figure 7-07

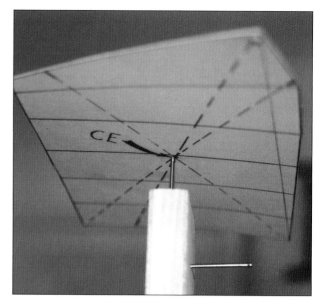

Figure 7-08

If the builder is replacing another sail with the Chinese lug sail or placing it on a boat showing no sail, a review of chapter 4 will prove useful. In order to either replace or place a sail, it will be necessary to find the COE of the Chinese lug sail. The author prefers to treat the Chinese lug sail like a standard four-sided sail, ignoring the roach at the leach or luff, and find the center of effort as discussed in chapter 4 (**Figure 7-07**). Van Loan uses stiff paper to make a scale model of the sail, and a pin to find the balance point, as in **Figure 7-08**. Hasler uses a more complicated method. Using stiff paper cut into a scale model, place a pinhole very close to the tack, clew, and peak. The hole should be large enough to allow the scale model to hang freely. Then, on a vertical surface, hang the paper sail from each pinhole, attach a string with a weight, and draw a line where the string falls (**Figures 7-09 a, b, c, d**). The intersection of the three lines will be the center of effort of the designed sail. The author tried all three methods on the same sail, and the results in **Figure 7-10** shows there is really no difference in the results of the three methods. For the owner having a single sail, any of the three methods will work just fine. However, the builder using more than one sail will need to use the system discussed in chapter 4 for finding the combined center of effort of all the sails.

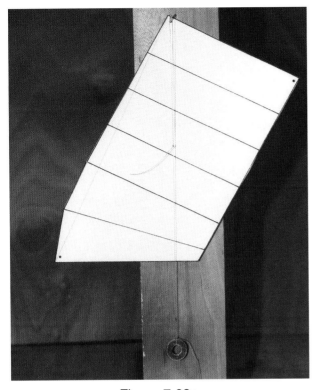

Figure 7-09a

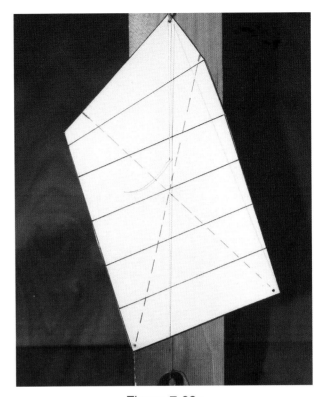

Figure 7-09c

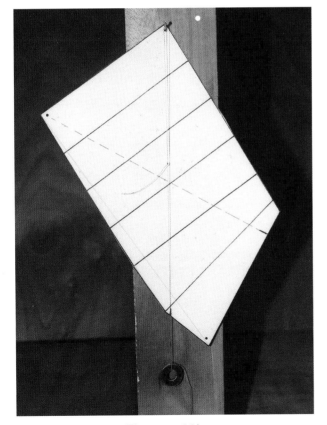

Figure 7-09b

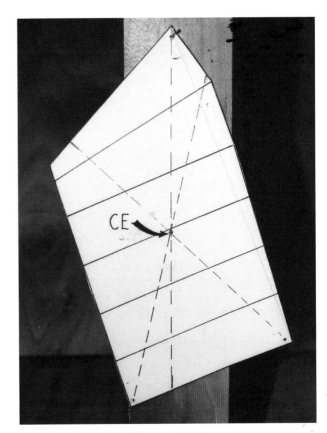

Figure 7-09d

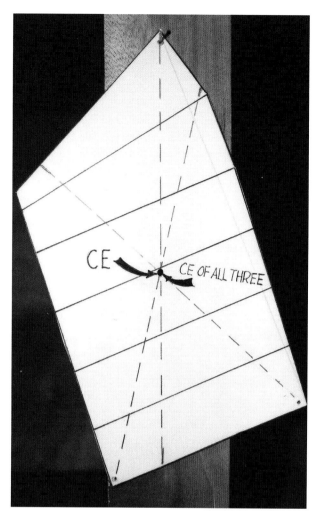

Figure 7-10

With the COE of the new Chinese lug sail established, it's just a matter of placing the new COE over the old COE to find the location of the new mast and sail. It is good to remember that the COE of the new sail is, in reality, a constantly changing point; the COE arrived at on the scale model is only an average at best. With that in mind, it will be wise to allow for some adjustment of the sail and mast.

Being able to move the sail fore and aft easily is just one of the many advantages of the Chinese lug sail. As noted earlier, a change in the amount of balance moves the COE—but there is another means open to the owner of the Chinese lug sail. The lack of standing rigging allows the rake of the mast to be easily adjusted as well.

While the Bermudian sailing rig almost always shows an aft rake of the mast the Chinese lug sail benefits from being very near vertical or with a slight rake forward. The slight rake forward will cause the sail to swing out, away from the centerline of the boat. This will be helpful when ghosting along because the sail doesn't have to be braced out to catch the light breeze. Even ghosting, the sail is self-tending.

Actually, the mast can be raked fairly far forward. This is particularly true for a two-masted rig where the forward sail is the smaller of the two. An examination of photos of Asian Chinese lug sails indicates that this is fairly common for the foresail. Hasler designed at least two boats (*Yeong* and *Batwing*) with a fairly substantial forward rake to the foresail. While a radical forward rake is strange to eyes accustomed to masts that rake aft, it can be very useful in shifting the COE of the sail and therefore adjusting the balance of the boat's helm.

This kind of adjustment is just one of many virtues of the Chinese lug sail, but there are downsides, not the least of which is complexity. Even the basic sail in **Figure**

7-01 has a large number of parts. The rigging for the sheets alone for this sail is significant. The sheets and sheet spans, along with the necessary blocks, represent a large outlay in money even if the builder makes his or her own blocks.

Then there is the time required to work out the rigging of the sheets and sheet spans. Working from a scale drawing will help determine the lengths of the rope, but the builder can count on time spent tweaking and debugging the system on the actual sail. Add to this the time needed to find the correct placement for the parrels and topping lifts, as well as the halyard, and it becomes obvious this is not a plug-and-play sail.

Also, on a small boat where the sail is removed each time, this will not only increase the setup time but also requires management under way. This can make sailing quickly become "line management." All the running rigging will require a designated place or container for storage to keep the inside of the boat from being covered with what will seem like miles of spaghetti.

While it is the running rigging that makes the sail so self-tending, it also contributes to what may be its main Achilles' heel. Hasler describes this as a "fan-up." A fan-up occurs when a partially or fully reefed sail is jibed with a strong wind directly aft and the sheets slack. The wind catches the top panels and unfolds the sail like a fan putting the yard in front of the mast. This can foul the rigging and lead to a serious problem.

Practical Junk Rig devotes several pages to fan-ups and details how to avoid them. *The Chinese Sailing Rig* doesn't mention them, even in passing. It is possible that fan-ups happen so infrequently that Van Loan didn't feel it was necessary to discuss them in his book.

However, if the builder is willing to live with fan-ups and take steps to avoid them, that basically leaves the sail's complexity as the main disadvantage. For many this complexity would not be a disadvantage at all. For those sailors, the Chinese lug sail presents an opportunity to have a sail easily handled under the worst conditions as well as the best of conditions.

8

GAFF SAILS

For many sailors the gaff sail is the quintessential traditional sail. It is the sail they've seen on catboats, schooners and working craft from the turn of the 20th century. It even appears in films like *Captains Courageous*, where all the fishing schooners were gaff-rigged. In fact the footage shot on the Grand Banks for this 1937 film is some of the last and best footage of the New England fishing fleet. Shots of those magnificent ships charging through the sea under full press of sail, decks awash, is part of what makes that film the wonderful classic it is.

Gaff sails move large heavy ships through the water very well, but those magnificent ships have miles of standing and running rigging. Even "little ships" like Thomas Gillmer's 22-foot Blue Moon, Fenwick Williams's 24-foot gaff yawl Anne, Paul Gartside's 22- and 18-foot trailerable cruisers, and Phil Bolger's 25-foot

Stone Camel must carry their fair share of standing and running rigging. All of the lovely gaff-rigged boats mentioned use running backstays as well, which are, in the words of one experienced sailor of gaff rigs, "A crashing bore."

But it is possible to use the gaff sail without all the attendant standing rigging. A number of designers like Charles Wittholz, Ted Brewer, Jay Benford, and Phil Bolger as well as several fiberglass manufacturers all have small to medium catboats that don't use all the standing rigging. Bolger has several large boats like the 39-foot Le Cabotin that use the gaff cat rig, as well.

But it's the boats in the size range of the 18-foot-2-inch fiberglass American Catboat, sailed by the author on Block Island Sound, Bolger's Chebacco and Wittholz's 11-foot dinghy that are of interest in this chapter. All these boats, even though they vary in size, have basically the same rig. In fact, when you strip away all the standing rigging, the sail is fairly simple.

Making the jaws of the gaff may prove the most complex part of this relatively simple sail. **Figure 8-01** shows an example of wooden jaws that turn slightly upward and have eyes for the throat halyard and attaching the throat of the sail. In the distant past this piece was grown to shape, however, today it will be necessary to laminate it from hardwood to achieve the curve upward.

There is also a block of hardwood that

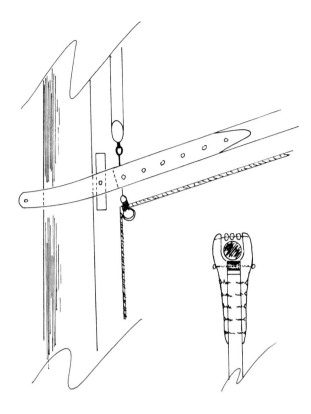

Figure 8-01

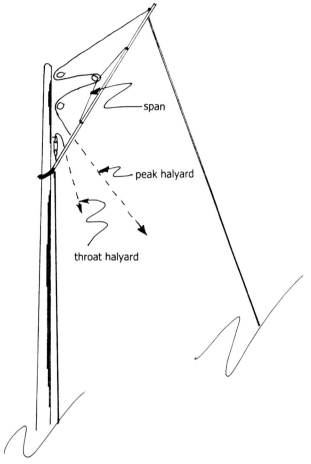

Figure 8-02

pivots with the gaff and remains flat against the mast. According to John Leather in *Gaff Rig* (International Marine, Camden Maine), this will be needed on sails exceeding 200 square feet. This small block takes the compression of the gaff, and it may be best to include the block on sails exceeding 100 square feet.

It's also suggested in *Gaff Rig* that the jaws be leathered on larger sails to reduce chafe. Whether the jaws are leathered or not, great care will be need to be taken to achieve the proper fit around the mast. It will be best to have the jaws extend past the mast and have space for parrel beads to keep the gaff captive against the mast. The prudent owner will step the mast and do

several dry runs in order to get the correct fit of the jaws. It will be good to allow for twist in the fit, as well.

Tom Cunliffe in *Hand, Reef and Steer* (Sheridan House, Dobbs Ferry, New York), reminds the owner that the throat halyard must lie parallel to the mast. This means that the top half of the throat halyard will need to be the same distance from the mast as where it attaches to the gaff. He also mentions that using a span system with the peak halyard will be "the kindest" to the gaff. The peak halyard system in **Figure 8-02** was used on the gaff-rigged catboat sailed by

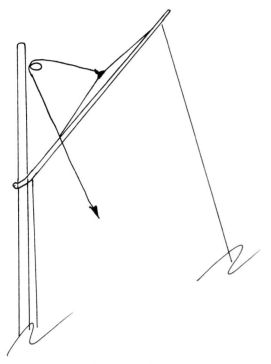

Figure 8-03

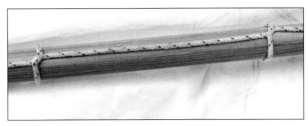

Figure 8-04

the author, but looking at old photographs shows an amazing variety of systems. In general, there seems to be no standard way of rigging the peak halyards; whatever worked was used. On very small sails, a span and saddle or block (**Figure 8-03**) would work and keep the amount of line to a minimum. Obviously, the larger the sail, the greater the purchase the peak halyard will need.

Whatever system is used, the span will need to be put on at the same time the head of the sail is bent on the gaff. There are a number of ways to bend on the sail, as well. Robands will certainly be the simplest method but probably not the best. Of the lacing methods, the marlin hitch (**Figure 8-04**) will keep the head of the sail snug against

the gaff and still allow for it to be kept tight.

Of all the ways to bend the sail onto the mast, hoops are one of the better choices. Aside from the aesthetic appeal, they aren't as prone to jam as some other methods. Seizing a light line to each hoop will help keep them parallel and even less jam prone (**Figure 8-05**). For small sails or boats on a trailer this will be easiest done with the sail raised on a windless day. Testing the system several times by raising and lowering the sail will always be a good idea.

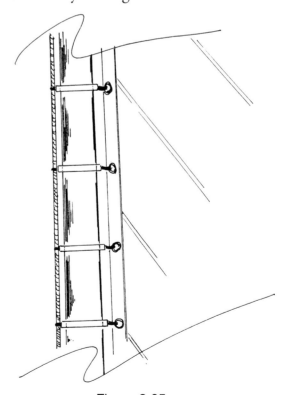

Figure 8-05

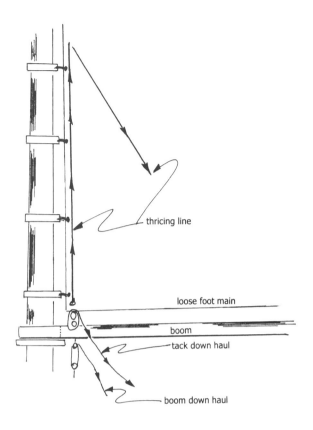

Figure 8-06

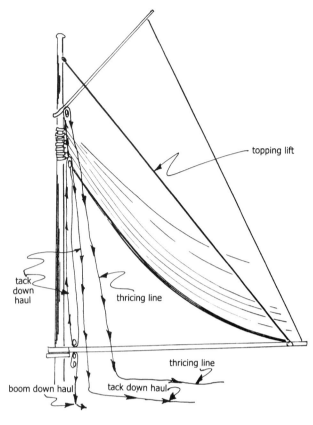

Figure 8-07

The downside to hoops is that the mast must be unstepped in order to take the sail off or on, but using a split hoop will overcome this minor problem. Split hoops will be most helpful on boats that are sailed off a trailer.

Using toggles with parrel beads is a system that can be easily made by the owner with rope and marlinspike skills. Adding a light line seized to each toggle much as in **Figure 8-05** will go a long way in helping to prevent jams as the sail is dropped. And while robands and various lacing methods will work, toggles or hoops may be the better choices for attaching the luff to the mast.

While the sail needs to be attached along the entire length of the luff and the head, the foot of the sail will be best left loose. Certainly it must be attached at the tack and the clew, but there are several ways of doing that.

One method involves attaching the tack to the boom with a downhaul rather than permanently seizing it on. Another line is then seized to the tack and fed upward along the mast to the jaws and then down again (**Figure 8-06**). By letting go the downhaul and pulling in the thricing line the tack is pulled upward toward the gaff jaws (**Figure 8-07**). Thricing up a sail almost completely de-powers it, or it can be thriced up in stages, which will slowly

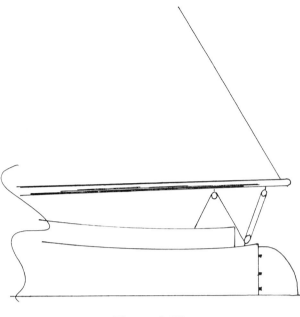

Figure 8-08

reduce the power of the sail. Reverse the process and the sail is back at full power in no time. Cunliffe, in *Hand, Reef and Steer*, speaks very highly of thricing as a means to lose way and control the boat.

The ability to thrice up a sail can be incredibly useful particularly in a catboat, which can be somewhat difficult to reef. This process requires two more additions to the boom: a topping lift, which should be there anyway, and a downhaul attached to the boom at the jaws (**Figure 8-07**). On large boats the weight of the boom will be sufficient hold it on the mast collar, but light booms will require a downhaul. It will not take a very large sail to need a purchase on the downhaul. In most cases, with small sails the downhaul can be made from thimbles seized into rope.

The mainsheet, however, will require

blocks so the sheet can run easily. How much of a purchase will depend on the size of the mainsail. **Figure 8-08** is the sheeting arrangement on the American Catboat for a 260-square-foot-sail. The author would have preferred a bit more purchase on the mainsheet, particularly when it breezed up, but that is a personal preference. How the blocks are laid out and how much purchase seems to be as individual as the boats and what the owner is comfortable with. In other words, there is no standard way to rig the mainsheet.

Being able to rig a sail in a manner that works best for the boat owner rather than a predetermined set of rules or conventions is one of the main attractions for traditional sails. In this same spirit of combining what works well, Phil Bolger and Friends have drawn several designs with what they have named a "Chinese Gaffer." The rig is really just a gaff sail with the battens, downhauls, and vangs of the Chinese lug sail. Yonder, a 30-foot long range cat yawl, and the 20-foot Singlehander, also a cat yawl, lead the vangs or sheets from the battens to the mizzenmast. The designers feel the sail combines the best qualities of the Chinese lug and the gaff sail.

Like all traditional sails the gaff sail lends itself to adaptation and change. From the schooners of *Captains Courageous* to the heavy workboats of Britain and America, to small pleasure dinghies, each boat or ship was rigged according to the owner's personal preference and experience. And the rigs on most of these boats and ships were "works in progress," being constantly tweaked and refined to better meet the needs of the owners.

9

VARIATIONS ON SEVERAL THEMES

The leg-of-mutton sail represents a traditional sail that is just a Bermudian sail without all the attendant standing rigging. This sail was used on a wide variety of working sailboats, particularly where the winds could be light. Charles G. Davis in a 1922 *Rudder* publication suggests the tall, thin sail added only a small amount of heeling, and in calm air the upper portion of the sail could extend up into moving air. This gave the leg-of-mutton a slight edge over a lower sail that might be becalmed. It was used extensively on sharpies all along the eastern seaboard; a variation was used on the Block Island Cowhorn as well.

A good many of these boats were large, 30 feet or more, like the New Haven tonging sharpie in the Mystic Seaport Museum's collection. These large boats were able to carry masts and sails tall enough to reach above calm air.

But even for the small boat, the leg-of-mutton sail's simplicity certainly makes it worth considering. With the sail permanently bent on the mast, there is nothing more than mast, sail, and mainsheet (**Figure 9-01**). This is about as basic as a rig can be. Also, because the sail has no standing rigging, there is less hull stress and less weight aloft—but this is an advantage of many traditional sails.

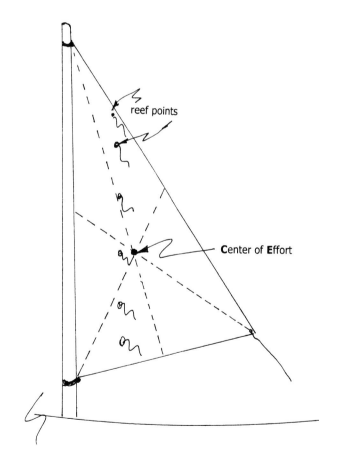

reef points

Center of **Effort**

Figure 9-01

In addition, without a boom, this sail can be shortened using a vertical reef as in **Figure 9-02**. One or more rows of cringles can be used and still have the basic sail of **Figure 9-01**. Of course, taking a reef on the luff will move the center of effort of the sail and change the balance of the helm. **Figure 9-02** shows that the COE of the reefed sail is forward and down from the old COE. Lowering the COE will help reduce the heeling of the boat; moving it forward will increase the lead, which will reduce weather helm up to a point. However, care will have to be taken to ensure that the boat doesn't develop unwanted lee helm as a result of too much lead.

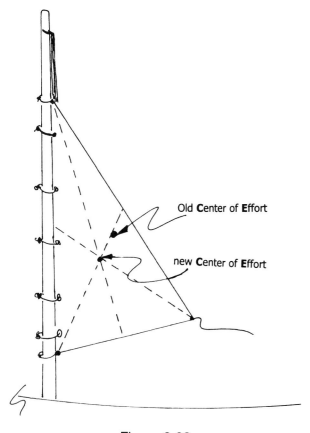

Figure 9-02

Having the sail permanently attached to the mast and reefing the luff has the additional advantage of eliminating the halyard. This has several positive effects other than just removing a line from the boat. Phil Bolger points out in *100 Small Boat Rigs* (International Marine) that without the halyard the mast can be thinner at the top. This reduces the weight and windage of the rigging aloft, and of course there are fewer items that have to be purchased.

This will be more practical with a small sail and mast that can be easily unstepped for reefing. Like many traditional sails that are extremely simple, tying in a reef will be best done on shore. Just beach the boat, unstep the sail, tie in the reef, and restep the mast. If a second mast partner farther aft has been put in the boat, then the balance of the helm will be unaffected by the reef. Multiple mast locations were common on working sailboats and can be very useful in small pleasure boats, as well.

All the simplicity does come at a price, however. The lack of a boom makes rigging and reefing simple but complicates sheeting the sail. Bolger also says, ". . . the ideal sheeting point moves with every change of course and conditions over a large area extending far outside the boat." The owner must decide if the simplicity is worth a sail that will not have the most efficient shape a good deal of the time. If the answer is no, then a boom will need to be added.

With the boomless sail, the clew will move up and out as the boat comes off the wind, and just adding a boom to the foot will not necessarily solve this problem. This sail will need to have the foot cut up to keep the boom out of the water on a reach. This high cut foot was common among the sailing dories and dinghies and does little to keep the clew down. The 21-foot Beachcomber sailing dory and the Herreshoff 11-foot dinghy both show this high-cut foot in the sail plans.

However, putting a sprit boom on the sail (**Figure 9-03**) will solve this and other problems because the sprit is self-vanging, as discussed in chapter 5, on the sliding gunter sail. Also, it's the self-vanging ability of the sprit that eliminates the need for

a purchase on the sheet. Bolger suggests that sails "up to 150 square feet can be sheeted without any mechanical advantage." Not having to deal with blocks on the mainsheet will make life in a small boat much more pleasant, not to mention less painful. And the sheeting point can be placed where it's more convenient because where the sail is sheeted is much less critical—however, the farther aft, the better.

Like other sails with a sprit boom the leg-of-mutton sail can be cut with more draft or camber to the sail. In light winds the snotter can be eased to give the sail more shape but pulled flat when the winds pipe up. A snotter rigged like **Figure 9-03** will allow for this kind of adjustment. While the adjustable snotter on the sprit boom will allow for the sail shape to be tweaked, it will chafe against the sail on one tack. Unless it's important to wring every ounce of speed from the boat, this will have little effect.

Those unwilling to live with the sprit pressing into the sail on one tack can always use a wishbone boom (**Figure 9-04**). Like most additions, there is a trade-off in complexity. The wishbone boom keeps all the fine-tuning abilities of the sprit but will require more running rigging as well as

Figure 9-03

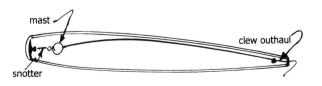

Figure 9-04

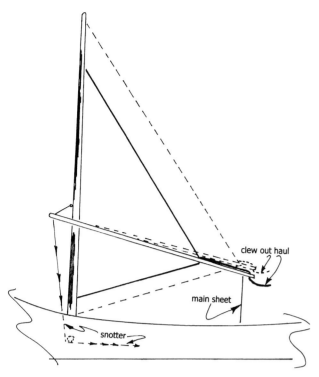

Figure 9-05

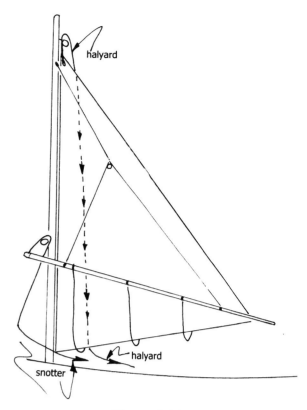

Figure 9-06

topping lifts. The sail can still be kept bent on the mast and reefs taken in the luff rather than the foot, but some sort of jiffy-reefing or brailing lines will be required. Also, a line will need to be made fast to the clew so it can move forward as the sail is reefed (**Figure 9-05**). With or without the wishbone the foot will need to be beefed up with extra tabbing and cut like it was on a boom. This is because there is always tension on the foot of the sail.

Another alternative is to add a halyard and use lazy jacks on the bottom of the wishbone to capture the reefed sail (**Figure 9-06**). This is a system that can be found on several production fiberglass boats.

A number of years back, this author had a conversation with the owner of a

Nonesuch 33, docked in Port Townsend, Washington. The Nonesuch 33 has a cat rig with a wishbone boom. This particular boat regularly sailed Puget Sound and the Pacific Ocean side of Vancouver Island either solo or short-handed.

This sailor loved his boat, but when he spoke about the wishbone boom his voice took on the tone of religious fervor. Here was an owner absolutely convinced this was the only sailing rig worth having; he firmly believed it would soon replace the standard Bermudian rig as soon as more owners found out about the wishbone. He quickly listed the sail's advantages like a man deeply in love, which he was. Short

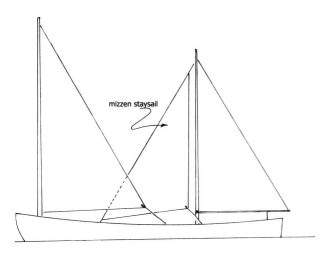

Figure 9-07

tacking was just a matter of laying over the helm. On a reach there was no need to sweat down and struggle with a boom vang (the sail was self-vanging). Jibing was as stress-free as tacking, and reefing, even solo, was just a matter of releasing the halyard and hauling in the downhaul. It was so easy, so simple. Here was where his voice became most passionate and his religious-like zeal was most apparent.

It might be best to temper this testimonial with Bolger's observation that in a heavy sea wishbone booms have a tendency to slam into the mast unless held with a very tight snotter, and they are "at their best in small and casual daysailers."

The leg-of-mutton does lend itself to rigs having more than one mast, like the cat ketch, and this gives the small boat several advantages. As on many of the working boats, using two masts allows for a large area of sail to be set and then struck

as the wind increases. **Figure 9-07** shows a boat rigged as a cat ketch and a mizzen staysail set. The mainsail is boomless, and the mizzen has a boom. Without a boom on the main, the staysail doesn't have to be lowered on each tack. The main will slide across the staysail like a jib.

This configuration would allow a small boat, 16 to 18 feet, the ability to ghost along with light winds. When the wind starts to increase the staysail could be quickly lowered. From there the main and mizzen can be juggled for the appropriate sail area and wind speed. However, being caught unaware by a sudden gust or increase in wind could have very unpleasant consequences, so a careful weather eye would need to be kept.

The idea of using more than one mast can be very appealing in a small boat, and the combinations possible are really quite large. The advantages of being able to set a staysail shouldn't be underestimated. The main problem the builder will have is not changing the balance of the boat's helm.

Maintaining the correct balance is not as hard as it might seem. The builder will just need to make careful scale drawings. A review of chapter 3 would be in order.

The main question would have to be: Is the versatility of a main and mizzen worth all the effort involved with extra sails and masts? The boat in **Figure 9-07** can spread a great deal of sail and strike it equally fast,

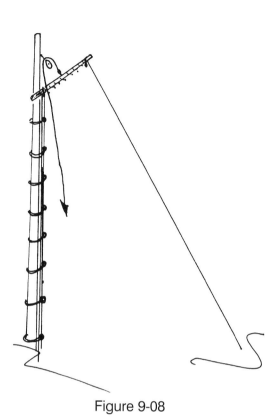

Figure 9-08

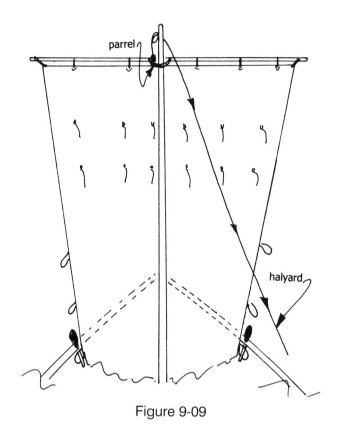

Figure 9-09

and there were many working boats that carried just that rig.

The Block Island Cowhorn in the collection of the Mystic Seaport Museum used almost exactly that configuration with a small change to the top of the sail. A small club was added at the head of the sail (**Figure 9-08**). The club allows the mast to be shorter and still have enough width at the top of the sail for some shape and uses a single halyard.

The leg-of-mutton and other traditional sails were designed to sail on all points of sail, but there is one sail used on Vistula Bay in Poland that is a downwind sail. In *WoodenBoat* #122 (January-February 1995), Aleksander Celarek describes the

sail used by Barkas fishing boats for trawling. While this sail was used on boats 30 to 50 feet in length, it does have some application on small boats.

To use this sail, the boat would have to have a freestanding mast rigged with a halyard. A simplified version of the Polish sail (**Figure 9-09**) is bent to a yard that has a parrel for the mast, and loops are sewn to each side of the sail at equal intervals. The loops are slipped on a belaying pin at the rail (**Figure 9-10**) and the halyard, which would have to act as a running backstay, is hauled tight. To shorten the sail, just ease the halyard, put a higher loop on the pin at each rail, and haul in the halyard.

According to Celarek, the sail is used

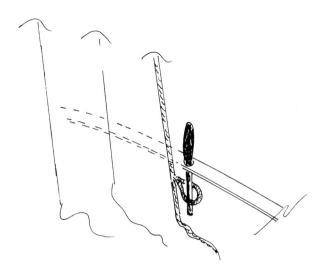

Figure 9-10

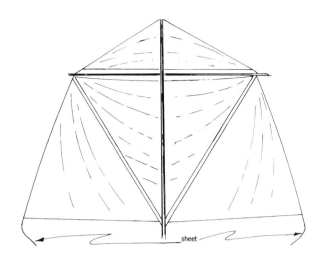

Figure 9-11

running and reaching while the Barkas trawl. While a small pleasure boat wouldn't be dragging a trawl, it does provide an interesting possibility for a boat with traditional sails to set a downwind sail similar to but far more simple than a spinnaker.

In fact a fairly large amount of sail could be set and if necessary struck quickly just by letting go the halyard. It seems it would be best if the yard didn't exceed the beam of the boat by much and the mast wasn't stepped in the very bow of the boat. The sail could be stored in the boat furled on the yard, and when the main sailing rig was struck, the Barkas sail set.

Reefing the sail against the yard would allow the yard to extend beyond the beam of the boat, giving the sail a trapezoidal shape. The sail could be shortened with loops down to the point where it was wider than the beam, and then reefs could be taken against the yard. Celarek's drawings

shows reef cringles that would allow reefs to be taken that way, and his illustrations seem to indicate a trapezoid shape to the sails so there is no reason to assume it wouldn't work on a smaller scale.

Some experimenting would be required, perhaps using inexpensive blue tarps, to see if the boat would lend itself to this type of sail and to find the proper pin placement. The owner not bound by one-design or racing rules could, with a little effort, have a great but very simple downwind sail.

A similar but more complex sail was designed by naval architect Jay Benford. Named "the Great Pyramid Rig" and described in his book *Cruising Yachts* (published by Tiller Press), this sail uses several large triangles of cloth set on a horizontal yard (**Figure 9-11**). This rig was originally used on a 34-foot Pinky Ketch and set 1,000 square feet of sail divided among the four individual sails but, like the Barkas

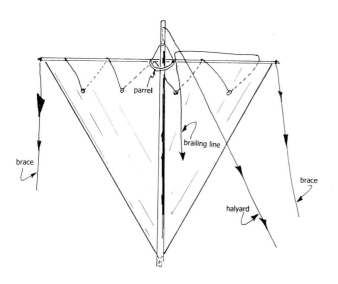

Figure 9-12

sail, it could be adapted to a small boat.

By just using the main and largest triangle, the small boat could set a sizable lightweight sail on a yard that would still store inside the boat. The halyard would need to act as a running backstay, and braces would be needed to control the rotation of the yard (**Figure 9-12**). Lines to brail the sail to the yard as the halyard is eased would reduce the sail area and lower the center of effort.

Certainly "the Great Pyramid" and the Barkas sail, if braces were added, would lend themselves to a boat with a mizzenmast. Braces run to the top of the mizzen and then down to the helm would keep the cockpit less cluttered and give a better angle for the braces.

Both sails would provide the small boat carrying a traditional rig a downwind sail that would be similar to a spinnaker. But unlike the spinnaker, which is all or nothing, both these sails could be reduced a little at a time. Also, aside from the halyard acting as a running backstay, the small versions of "the Great Pyramid" and Barkas sails would be missing all the standing rigging and the whisker pole required by the spinnaker.

It is the very lack of standing rigging that will require the owner to exercise caution in determining the size of these sails. A downwind sail that is too large can break an unstayed mast or cause damaging stress to the hull. And the prudent sailor might want to add a downhaul on the yard for more positive control when striking the sail.

However, both of these sails would complement the leg-of-mutton and its variants —or any of the other traditional sails, for that matter. For the owner willing to experiment, traditional sails can work together so the boat can be fitted with the perfect combination of efficient yet simple sails, sails that don't require standing rigging, whisker poles, or other expensive gear that must be purchased—sails that the owner can rig as well as repair, and that complement the spirit and appearance of the boat.